IF AT FIRST YOU DON'T SUCCEED

The Life Story of Ron Lea

Family man, farmer, race driver, entrepreneur, traveller & bon viveur

Published by

An Imprint of Melrose Press Limited
St Thomas Place, Ely
Cambridgeshire, CB7 4GG, UK
www.melrosebooks.com

FIRST EDITION

Cover designed by Jeremy Kay

ISBN 978-1-908645-0-29

Printed and bound in Great Britain by:
TJ International Ltd, Padstow, Cornwall

MIX
Paper from responsible sources
FSC www.fsc.org FSC® C013056

Contents

IF

by Rudyard Kipling

If you can keep your head when all about you
Are losing theirs and blaming it on you,
If you can trust yourself when all men doubt you,
But make allowance for their doubting too;
If you can wait and not be tired by waiting,
Or being lied about, don’t deal in lies,
Or being hated don’t give way to hating,
And yet don’t look too good, nor talk too wise:

If you can dream – and not make dreams your master;
If you can think – and not make thoughts your aim;
If you can meet with Triumph and Disaster
And treat those two imposters just the same;
If you can bear to hear the truth you’ve spoken.
Twisted by knaves to make a trap for fools.
Or watch the things you gave your life to, broken,
And stoop and build ’em up with worn-out tools.

If you can make one heap of all your winnings
And risk it on one turn of pitch and toss,
And lose, and start again at your beginnings
And never breathe a word about your loss;
If you can force your heart and nerve and sinew
To serve your turn long after they are gone,
And so hold on when there is nothing in you
Except the Will which says to them ‘Hold on’.

If you can talk with crowds and keep your virtue,
Or walk with Kings – nor lose the common touch,
If neither foes nor loving friends can hurt you,
If all men count with you, but none too much;
If you can fill the unforgiving minute
With sixty seconds worth of distance run,
Yours is the earth and everything that’s in it,
And – which is more – you’ll be a Man, my son!

Preface

The scope of this autobiography covers highlights of the author's eventful life but not his most personal adult family connections. In particular, it is aimed at those young people who are starting out in adulthood when the pressures of life seem insurmountable. IF AT FIRST YOU DON'T SUCCEED, TRY, TRY AGAIN.

This quotation is not from the poet Rudyard Kipling, but his famous poem 'If' covers many of the tribulations to which I was subjected myself, beginning with the first verse which covers my experience in the family company under the chapter headed 'Clogs to Clogs in Three Generations'. The second verse covers the experience of starting a new independent business with all its 'ups and downs' and the third verse the trauma created by the actions of third parties in an established project which was about to fulfil an early retirement. Finally, the last verse reminds me that after more than thirty-five years as a member of the Jaguar Drivers' Club, which was founded in 1956, initially to promote motorsport, and which at the time of writing has no involvement in motor racing whatsoever due to the self-interest of certain officials of the JDC and the Jaguar Car Club. I am also a member of the Jaguar Enthusiasts' Club because they have taken over the promotion of Jaguar club motorsport.

This life story covers early family life, sporting success and disappointment, overseas travel both personal and following my motor racing hobby, practical farming both in the UK and the USA, National Service in the Army, developing and losing through criminal conspiracy several successful companies both in the UK and Belgium. Throughout I was supported by my wife, Sheila, both in administration and care.

Having written articles for the *Jaguar Driver* magazine for many years under the headings of 'Competition News', 'Wide Angle' and 'Historic Replicar News', on two occasions I wrote monthly about personal motor racing experiences for both the *Jaguar Driver* and the *Jaguar Enthusiast* magazines including as a spectator from the late 1940s and as an amateur club competitor from 1977 at the age of forty-six years, always in Jaguar cars. During this latter period, probably because of my business experience and being a late starter, I tended to become involved in the administration of Jaguar-oriented motorsport, and this was highlighted by the award of the prestigious accolade Jaguar Driver of the Year in 1983 by Sir John Egan. The commendation included reference to both success on the track and administration whereas previously this annual award went to successful racers only worldwide.

My own racing successes are listed in this autobiography, as are the details of the organisation and promotion I was involved in including

Ron on buggy with Sheila
(Photograph by Brian Ekin)

the Cheshire Cats Trophy meeting at Oulton Park, the Jaguar team in the AMOC Intermarque Challenge championship, the Paladin Shield Historic Replicar championship, later to become the Sports Racing & GT series, the Historic Replicar Register of the Jaguar Drivers' Club, the Sir William Lyons Inter-Club Relay Challenge and finally, the England/Hawthorn Memorial Appeal for a composite statue erected in the Brooklands Garden at Goodwood with the kind permission of the Earl of March.

As an octogenarian and the victim of a debilitating stroke in 1996, I decided to continue my life-long interest in motorsport, but this time as an entrant only, and so completing my involvement as a Spectator, Competitor, Administrator, Promoter and finally as a Sponsor/Entrant with my supercharged D-Type replica in Powered by Jaguar events in 2012.

However, as this race car was built for myself to compete in motorsport if I had not had a stroke, there is little doubt that this literary work would never have been started, but the enforced immobility enabled me to begin by dictating on a personal recorder, which my wife typed up, until later when I obtained Dragon Naturally Speaking voice-recognition software for the computer, and dictated the story direct; but when my voice became tired the recording became distorted. I therefore continued to type on a word processor with the finger of one hand until the strain resulted in a 'trigger finger' which was operated on by an orthopaedic surgeon. I was therefore grateful that a local part-time medical secretary, Mrs Gill Howard, was able to complete the story. I hope readers will find these efforts worthwhile and interesting.

RON LEA

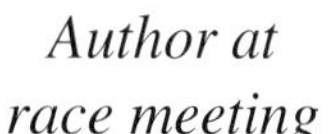

Author at
race meeting

CHAPTER 1

Early Family Life

I was born on the 18th of April 1931 at 9 Ashbourne Grove, Whitefield, near Bury, Lancashire. I was born with a rash because my mother had caught measles during her pregnancy. Fortunately, it was not the German variety which has a record of giving pregnant women deformed babies. Cockneys are proud to say they were born within the sound of Bow Bells. When asked as a proud Lancastrian, I would say I was born within the sound of Besses o' th' Barn Band, a famous brass band in the area.

My father, Harry Lea, was a grandson of the founder (1869) of Joseph Lea & Sons Limited, Dyche Street, Rochdale Road, Manchester, and worked in the family firm most of his life. My mother, Lillian Needham, was one of a family of seven. Her father was a well known antique dealer, John Walter Needham of Deansgate Arcade, Manchester. My father died in 1994 aged ninety years, my mother in 1973 aged seventy years.

My mother Lillian Lea (née Needham)

Although she lived for the biblical three-score-and-ten, she had an undiagnosed illness towards the end of her life which her GP could not fathom. Her ancestors had a record of long life. I therefore made arrangements with a customer to rent her his flat in Tenerife for rehabilitation, but she declined the offer. I was also advised of a person living in Cornwall, Mr A. J. Edwards, who had a reputation for successfully diagnosing and curing people with similar symptoms and I wrote to him in October 1972 advising that if he could help, I would bring her down at short notice. I received an immediate reply from Mrs Edwards advising that he no longer practised due to illness.

I will always be grateful to her for her determination that my breakaway from the family company in 1967 would not jeopardise the family relationship, at which she was 100% successful in that there was a reconciliation with my father soon after.

I was nine years old when the Second World War started in 1940 and prior to this, I was known as a high spirited and rebellious child, so much so that I was sent to school aged three years when the normal starting age was five years. Whilst my father was a severe disciplinarian and believed in corporal punishment, my mother was very much a believer in guidance and realised I could be led, but not driven. Both these upbringing psychologies helped to form my character. I was nicknamed 'Titch' from an early age.

Lea family - Left to right: Ron, Lillian, Christine, Harry and Peter

Nearby, there was a modern bungalow in which Roland Hall and his family lived. Roland Hall was the Managing Director of the famous family company Halls Sweets, with a factory in the centre of Whitefield. He was very keen on flying and had a reputation of being completely mad, so much so, that when he volunteered for the RAF, although he had his pilot's licence, he was allegedly turned down. However, it was prior to the 5th of November on Guy Fawkes Night that his support for the local bonfire was most appreciated. He not only bought a considerable number of fireworks, but had wooden boxes delivered to the site from his factory. This gave us a good starting point of dry flammable wood. Those who lived in the immediate area were called the 'Whitefield Gang' but there were few opportunities in this built-up area to find tree branches to build up the fire. Only about three miles away, however, there was another gang, the 'Nipper Lane Gang' who had their own bonfire and there began a series of raids prior to Bonfire Night in both directions to steal whatever branches could be tied to the back of bicycles. Sometimes gang members were intercepted and a fracas would develop.

My brother, Peter Lea, was born on 16th of April 1929 and although there were only two years between us, initially we had completely different sets of friends. In the area, there were numerous uncles, aunties and cousins. We would often see these relations, particularly at Christmas when my parents gave a party in which both sides of the family, the Leas and the Needhams, would get together and have a sing-song in No. 9 Ashbourne Grove. My father was a pianist and church organist, and my mother was very artistic, being a landscape oil painter and a classic contralto vocalist, a talent which our eldest daughter, Yvonne, has inherited. It was at these family parties I was encouraged to sing also, following which I would go round with my hat to collect three-penny bits.

Although I was very active, I did suffer from two major illnesses. I had diphtheria when I was seven years old: I was taken by ambulance to the Florence Nightingale Hospital in Bury. I took my teddy bear with me for comfort in the male adult ward, and when I would not eat the 'gritty' shepherd's pie that was served daily, the ward sister decided I required constant injections so that my bottom was like a pin cushion. Tragically, Teddy died in hospital because he was presumed infected. Shepherds pie has never been my favourite dish. Although I completely recovered, this disease always leaves its mark, and some years later, I became short-sighted and had to wear spectacles, the only one in the family.

Peter and Ron (Titch), back seat driver in first car

Whitefield Preparatory School: Titch hiding at the back!

The other ailment in this period was a stomach problem, undiagnosed until a German Jewish refugee, Dr Auerbach, gave me the most likely reason for the violent pain as an internal organ that had not grown during development. The pain was to cease a few years later. At times, attacks became quite serious and on one occasion on the train from Whitefield to Prestwich, it had to make an emergency stop for me to be taken to the Jewish Hospital by ambulance.

My sister, Christine, was born on 22nd of March, 1940. It was when I first saw the all-enveloping gas mask in which Christine was placed that I first became aware of the imminent danger of the war. Otherwise, this early war period was very exciting and interesting: collecting shrapnel, partly burnt-out incendiary bombs and swapping them for other collections with school mates.

The droning sounds of the German bombers overhead and the bombs exploding were of little concern and I recollect on the first night of the Manchester blitz being invited into my parents' bedroom to witness the raging fires at Salford docks, so bright that one could read a newspaper. After the second night of the blitz on Manchester, my parents were so concerned for our safety that they arranged with my mother's niece, Margery, and her husband, Keith Sargison, to come over in their car and collect my brother and myself and take us to Keith's mother's pub in Chorley. Although there were detours, we were able to see the devastation of Salford docks on the way. Just prior to this our father had taken us down to Manchester to see the burnt-out remains of the factory of Joseph Lea & Sons Limited where my father's younger brother, Geoffrey Lea, was seen trying to force open the burnt-out safe in which all the company papers were held.

It was following this that my parents decided that they had to get us out of the area for the duration of the war and contacted my mother's brother in the USA, Bill Needham, with a view to evacuation to his farm in New York State. Before the arrangements were completed, however, an evacuation ship, *City of Benares*, was torpedoed in the Atlantic and seventy-seven children were drowned. My parents considered, therefore, that the risk was too great, and it was not until nine years later when I was eighteen that I crossed the Atlantic to stay with my uncle and work on his farm.

Maternal grandfather, John Walter Needham

Paternal grandfather, John Lea

Lea/Needham 'get-together'

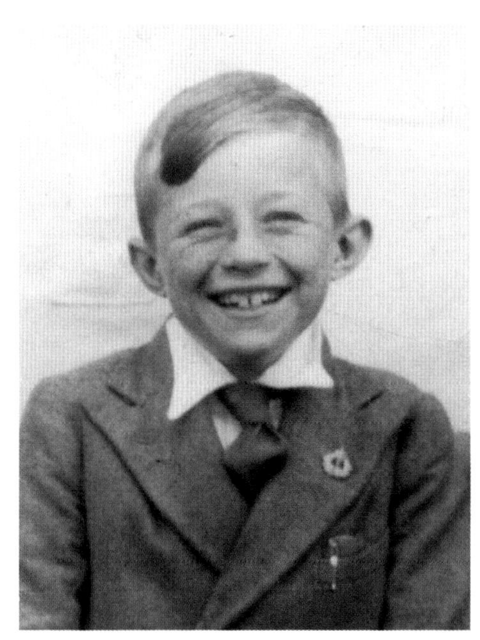

Titch the boisterous little devil!

Titch in beauty parade at Dovercourt Holiday Camp

A furious Titch persuaded to loan his new cowboy suit to another boy!

CHAPTER 2

This Was A Character-Forming Experience

My parents then decided that the only alternative was to send us to boarding school, and they approached the headmaster, Mr Defoe, at Queen Elizabeth School, Kirkby Lonsdale, Westmorland. Although normally pupils did not enter the school until they were eleven years old, Mr Defoe accepted me at nine years old because I would be joining my brother who was eleven years old and because of the special circumstances at the time. We started the first term at the end of 1940. Mr Defoe was the finest headmaster I ever came across in my school career. He was a strict disciplinarian interested in both the academic and sporting prowess of his pupils and planted the seed from which later developed a love of classical music culminating in my becoming a life member of the Hallé Concerts Society. Every Sunday evening without fail he held music sessions in the school library which all pupils had to attend. He played recorded classical music in which he would explain the styles of the great composers and bring to our notice music which otherwise would have fallen on deaf ears. He had, of course, favourite composers and was very much against swing and jazz. On one occasion he brought records of famous swing bands, played them for a short while and contrasted them with Mozart or Beethoven and then broke the new swing records to show his disdain. Perhaps it was a bit extreme, but there was no question of the point he was making.

Older brother Peter (Lanky) at Queen Elizabeth's School

I would have seen out my school career at Queen Elizabeth's if it were not for a problem of bullying. In retrospect, there is no doubt that bullying did occur, but one has to ask how much of it was brought about by the bullied person's own attitude. There is a difference between a 'tough' nine-year-old and a 'tough' eleven-year-old. There is no doubt that even at this early age, I believed I could look after myself and there was a certain amount of pride involved which stopped me from backing down when it was prudent to do so. However, it was an ongoing problem which together with homesickness, eventually led to my parents withdrawing me from this very good school. I was certainly not happy there and took every opportunity to escape from the environment, including joining the church choir in the village of Kirkby Lonsdale, persuading the headmaster that I was very keen on fishing and getting time off to fish in the River Lune and half-heartedly running away now and then. Every week in the summer pupils would go down to the River Lune to swim, supervised by one of the staff. It was on one of these occasions that I nearly drowned when I mistakenly tried to paddle (non-swimmer), not allowing for the shelving of the river bottom, and suddenly sank in several feet of water. It was some years later before I learned to swim after this experience.

Not only were there some interesting personalities amongst the school staff, but also among some of the senior pupils. It was co-educational and the girls had their own residential house and there were several attempts by older boys to make contact out of hours, one of whom was expelled after being caught inside. One of these boys, the Head Prefect, was expelled ostensibly for diving off the Devil's Bridge over the River Lune in a dare for a ten shilling bet. Appropriately named the Devil's Bridge, as any visitor will confirm after they have looked over the parapet, the jagged rocks on the river bed can be seen through the clear water and such a dive must have taken a lot of courage as well as accuracy in choosing the spot. The origin of the bridge's name goes back into antiquity when it was alleged that the Devil challenged an old peasant woman and her dog that whoever was the first to cross the bridge would be cursed. She very cleverly sent the dog ahead and so thwarted the devil's evil plot. The area around the bridge is a popular motorcycle meeting place. Although this was given as the reason I had my doubts at the time after I inadvertently found him having a rendezvous with the young Assistant Matron in the school washroom. Clearly this was not to be encouraged with staff.

The Devil's Bridge at Kirkby Lonsdale, Westmorland

Our parents used to visit us regularly at the weekends and quite often we would enjoy a 'slap up' meal at Mrs Slater's Public House at Arkholme. It was combined with a farm, run by her husband, which provided unlimited free range ham and eggs. It was a banquet in these stringent food ration times, especially for my brother and myself who were used to plain school fare. During the first summer, the army arrived opposite the school playing fields to erect concrete tank traps on the roads. The German invasion was expected at any time. They were men from the new

Parachute Regiment and I climbed over the wall of the playing fields to talk to one of the soldiers, a sergeant called 'Ginger', a gigantic man who turned out to be a PTI (Physical Training Instructor). He had been a champion heavyweight boxer and was very friendly. At the time, I was having a problem with one particular school bully so he gave me boxing lessons and urged me to take him on. (It was many years later that I read about Ginger Green at the Battle of Arnhem and after the Jaguar Drivers Club Rally to Geneva in 1986, my wife and I visited Arnhem and the Military Cemetery in case he had not survived the battle, but could not find his name recorded.)

It was at Queen Elizabeth School that my brother was given the nickname 'Lanky'. My nickname was 'Titch' because I was small and slight and Peter's because he was five feet ten inches tall at fourteen years of age.

At the end of term, we were taken to our new home at 4 Bramhall Park Road, Bramhall, Cheshire. It was during this holiday that I met members of the American army stationed at nearby Poynton, who were invited into the homes of several residents, including my parents. They all seemed to have Italian names and I particularly remember Frank Googliano and Amando Delsando. The latter was an interesting person to myself because he had been a professional boxer and a gangster in Prohibition days in the USA. After D-Day on the 6th June 1944, all these Americans left the area and were not seen again.

Sister Christine with Ron in garden at home in Bramhall Park Road

Next door to No. 4 lived a Mr and Mrs Marples and their daughter; their son was in the RAF and became a fighter ace during the Battle of Britain. I particularly remember his Spitfire arriving over Bramhall Park Road and doing acrobatics to the great excitement of Mrs Marples and her daughter and my mother and myself who all rushed out of the house to witness it. Soon after, Roy Marples, who had been withdrawn from active duty, was killed in a mid-air collision with a trainee Polish pilot.

I went to Queen Elizabeth School in July 1940 and left at the end of March 1943 and commenced at Stockport Grammar School in May of that year. No. 4 Bramhall Park Road was conveniently placed for the bus stop in Bramhall Lane and it

Jaguar SS100 sportscar which started the author's love of the marque (Photo by Alan Gibbins)

was whilst waiting for the bus that I often saw a black Jaguar SS100 drive past with two men in same, both with overcoats in the winter and both wearing trilby hats. I never saw the car with the hood erected. I could hear the rumble of this car as it came up the hill from Bridge Lane and looked forward to it passing almost every day. It was only later that I found out the driver was Mr Moore with his son who owned the well-known hat makers at Denton, near Manchester. This was the beginning of my love affair with the Jaguar marque, of which I eventually was to own several models and was to race for nearly twenty years.

It was some time later on the same bus route that a stranger approached me on the journey to ask if I was Ron Lea and if I would be interested in playing rugby football when I left school. He was an amateur talent scout for Davenport Rugby Club (now known as Stockport Rugby Club) and I have always remembered this short conversation because although playing for the school football first team at the time, I always expected to play rugby when I left school, which I had enjoyed as junior at Queen Elizabeth School. It seems my reputation as an athlete had got around!

The headmaster of Stockport Grammar School, Mr Philpot, was in complete contrast to Mr Defoe, headmaster at Queen Elizabeth School. Even so, it was a good school and I began to develop sporting prowess there, if not showing any academic ability. I was lazy and showed little interest in the latter and recollect practising cricket in the nets when one of the school masters, W. A. Payne, 'Willie Wapp', said to me, 'Lea, you would not bother coming to school if it wasn't for sport would you?' I took part in all forms of organised sport, but excelled in soccer and athletics. In fact, the most effective discipline to keep me in line was detention on Saturday afternoon supervised by Mr Conway, the Latin teacher, when you were expected to write on special letter formation paper which certainly improved my handwriting, but left me very frustrated at missing the afternoon sport.

Stockport Grammar School 1st eleven football team with Ron kneeling on right

There had been no detention at Queen Elizabeth's, but corporal punishment with the cane by the headmaster which, although painful at the time, certainly did not have the salutary effect of being kept in detention at Stockport Grammar. During the next few years, I excelled in athletics, winning the 100 yards, 200 yards and long jump and the *Victor Ludorum*. I also won the ATC East Cheshire Championship for 100 and 220 yards at Cosford in 1947 at the age of sixteen years. I was centre forward in the soccer First Team and was very interested in boxing and won the mid-weight championship when I 'hammered' a noted school bully. In fact, of course, it was my experience at Queen Elizabeth that made me particularly averse to any boy who showed these tendencies and now, of course, I could do something about it.

It was during one of the long holidays at this time that I was asked by Peter Rowlinson (who later founded the well known building company, Rowlinson's Constructions), the captain of the school First Team, to play a friendly match against Stockport County Reserves. It was during this game that I was to receive an injury which effectively finished my sporting aspirations. The tactical plan of the school team, used on more than one occasion, was for the inside left, Geoff Sellers, to pass the ball through the centre for me to run on to as I had very good acceleration and sprint speed. On this occasion, the opposing goalkeeper ran out to collect the ball and instead of diving on it to 'kill it', lost his nerve and fly-kicked, missing the ball but hitting my knee with such an impact that it broke two cartilages. Eventually, I had one of these cartilages removed by Mr Griffiths at the Manchester PPH but he had misdiagnosed the problem and only identified the cartilage on the inside of the knee whereas the cartilage on the outside was also torn. In the end, it was correctly diagnosed by Mr Harry Platt (Sir Harry when he died aged 100 years some time later) when I was only given a fifty-fifty chance of being able to walk without a stiff leg. Unfortunately, in retrospect, I did not take this risk and my sporting prospects came to an end.

On leaving school in 1947, I was at a loss to know what to do. My parents had moved house in July 1944 to the other end of Bramhall Park Road, Ladybrook Road, Cheadle Hulme. I therefore initially joined Joseph Lea & Sons Limited, the family firm, drilling dumb jacks with holes for grease nipples in the spring hangers and other light engineering work, because one of the main businesses was spring repairs and trailer manufacturers.

I did not stay long, however, and got my first proper job at a farm in Cheadle Hulme with Walter Curtis who also had another farm at Alderley Edge. This was a dairy farm with a herd of pedigree Friesians and the manager was Mr John Sloan. He was an experienced herdsman, but I particularly recollect the risk he took with a very large bull when he went into its pen and was caught in the corner and was lucky to escape with just a mutilated hand which became trapped on the wall by the bull's horns. They also had a draught horse which was looked after by one of the longstanding employees who certainly had no respect for it when I caught him urinating on the horse's fetlocks which could not have done it any good. On one occasion, I was asked to take the horse down to the farrier, Jack Spratt, riding bareback with just a rein. I was warned that if I heard a train coming I should get off the horse before crossing the bridge as it was likely to bolt!

TO WHOM IT MAY CONCERN
This is to certify that Ronald Victor Lea has been in my employ for the past six months, during which time I have been very pleased with the way he has done his work. He is honest, reliable and always willing to do all that is asked of him, and I have pleasure in recommending him for the position for which he is applying.
Walter Curtis

I was still undecided what I wanted to do and so I soon left the farm and started work at Wolfe & O'Meara in John Dalton Street, Manchester, Fine Furniture and Antique Dealers. I had hoped to join my grandfather, John Walter Needham, in Deansgate Arcade, but there seemed to be some family resistance to this as they already employed more than one of his own children and their spouses. I therefore left Wolfe & O'Meara's and got a job on Dunge Farm at Alderley Edge. I was still at the family home in Cheadle Hulme and initially I would walk the four miles down to Cheadle Hulme Station and get the milk train at 5.30 am and was met at Alderley Edge Station by George Bullock, the bailiff of Dunge Farm, in his van. This farm on the top of the 'Edge' was owned by Sir Geoffrey Parkes of Parkes & Nephew, Iron & Steel Stockholders. It was only a hobby to him and was a model farm with pedigree Jersey cows, all hand-milked. I became quite skilled at this basic job therefore, and developed muscles on the elbow of each arm due to the manipulation of the fingers, especially when the cow had warts on its teats and only the fourth finger and thumb could be used. It was here that I began to learn some basic farming jobs working with George Bullock, there being only the two of us on the farm.

The early train from Cheadle Hulme to Alderley did not carry on for long because my father bought me a 125cc Royal Enfield 'Flying Flea' motorcycle. I would travel the back way to the farm through Mottram St Andrews and on more than one occasion the headlight of my motorcycle seemed to attract bats, nocturnal creatures which dive-bombed me and bounced off my leather helmet! This was the least of my problems because, as usual, I rode too fast and it was fortunate that there was no other traffic on the roads at this time.

Later my father bought me a BSA B32 350cc motorcycle. I joined the Cheadle Hulme Motorcycling Club and went with other members on Sunday rides in the country which always ended in a race on the return journey. The secretary of the club decided that as I was always the first bike back, I should do some racing and introduced me to a motorcycle mechanic who had a double-knocker Norton and wanted to enter it in the Manx TT.

I did not pursue this possibility because, when I got my driving licence at seventeen years old, an interest in motor vehicles developed and I left Dunge Farm and became an apprentice mechanic. This was at Davenport Garage owned by Mr Christianson and Mr Eddie Bell, the latter was the owner of Bell's Brewery in Stockport and occasionally we had darts matches against the Bell's employees when I represented Davenport Garage. My interest in motorsport developed while I was there and I gained a reputation for being a quick and fearless driver, usually in my father's car. I was also developing an interest in bodybuilding and weightlifting now that active sport was excluded by my damaged leg.

Because of these developing attributes one day I was asked by Arthur, a salesman in the showroom at Davenport Garage, to come to the front and try to start a Rover car of early vintage by cranking the engine. Putting the starting handle through the grill, I wound the engine steadily, but without success. I had difficulty in removing the handle, but then found it was like a corkscrew! The engine had seized and my efforts to start it were of no avail, but it needed a replacement starting handle. My mechanical knowledge at this stage was very limited and as I had taken up weightlifting my new-found strength was very satisfactory to me. However, it did get me in some trouble because on another occasion, the works foreman asked me to tighten the head bolts on a customer's engine which had been de-coked and in the process I overtightened one of the bolts which broke off whilst the customer was watching me at work.

It was whilst employed at the garage that I went to watch the first British Grand Prix in 1948. This was held at Silverstone and was a very exciting occasion because the two Italian works Maserati 4CLT cars were late arriving from Italy and were to be driven by Luigi Villoresi and Alberto Ascari and had to start at the back of the grid with a ten-second penalty because they had not practised. One of my vivid recollections, therefore, was the two red 'bullets' coming through the field at very high speed to take first and second positions. In the pits at this time was another motor racing enthusiast, John Pearson, whom I was to get to know much later when I started motor racing myself and who became a good friend, and eventually a member of the organising committee for the England/Hawthorn Memorial.

1948 RAC Grand Prix at Silverstone: original painting by Nicholas Watts

CHAPTER 3

Go West Young Man

Although I was interest in farming I had not really been given an opportunity to learn the business, but only acted as a labourer. It was suggested by my mother that I join her older brother, Bill Needham, who was farming in New York state, where my brother and myself were very nearly evacuated to in the war. Bill Needham was a self-taught expert grassland farmer who specialised in the preparation of silage and, on occasions, he was asked to lecture at Cornell University. According to family legend, he ran away from home aged fifteen years with a pal and when they arrived at Liverpool docks, tossed a coin to decide whether to go to the USA or Australia as ships left for both destinations in those days. The 'States' won and after he arrived, he got a job on a farm in New York state.

Because his mother, my maternal grandmother Sarah Needham (née Barry), had not received any word from him whatsoever although she knew he was in America, she contacted the US Embassy and complained about her son's neglect in writing to her. Soon after, Bill was working in the farm field when he heard the sirens of police motorcycles escorting the Mayor's limousine which stopped abruptly next to him and the Mayor started to berate him for not writing to his mother! Typical American sentiment.

Consequently, before I left on this great adventure, my mother had impressed upon her brother that it was essential I return after a specific period, and when this was agreed, I boarded the *Britannic* ocean liner at Liverpool bound for New York on the 16th May 1949, aged eighteen. The crossing took seven days and I met many young people a little older than myself who were students and visitors to the UK and Europe and returning home. It was a very exciting trip which involved much boozing and light romance. On leaving Liverpool, the ship stopped at Cobh (Queenstown) where Irish immigrants boarded from a pilot boat in the river estuary. As I was berthed in steerage class, I got to know some of these emigrants. Time went very quickly as there was much to do on board including a 'contretemps' over a girl with a Canadian ice hockey player whose team was returning from playing in Europe. I won the table tennis championships on board and finally we arrived off New York harbour.

My first recollection was of the Statue of Liberty. I was surprised to see that it was green (I was to learn later that this was because it was copper plated) and as we passed this commemorative statute to 'God's own country' another surprise was to see the innumerable condoms (French letters as we knew them then) streaming down the river in the flowing tide. There had been a strike by pilot boat captains and staff at the time so that our captain had to manoeuvre this very large ship into its berth unaided, which he did successfully.

American Needham family, circa 1940.
Left to right: back row; Dorothy, Lillian, Phyllis, Margery: front row; Billy, Uncle Bill, Auntie Bernice, Caroline

As I stood on the forecastle of the ship watching these complicated manoeuvres, I spotted two people on the dockside. It was my uncle, Bill Needham, and the Sheriff of Newark Valley, Tioga County, who had agreed to drive my uncle to New York City. I remember shouting to them and receiving their reply to get off the ship 'pronto' as it was several hours late. It seemed that they had hoped to go to see the New York Yankees play baseball, but with the delay, the game had been missed. Instead we went for a drink in a downtown seedy bar which was full of negro dock workers. We then set off on the 300-mile journey in the sheriff's car, a Kaiser saloon (a manufacturer who had set up after the war, having gained a reputation for making the Liberty ships).

My own recollection of the journey now is of the appearance of the countryside which was similar to West Wales with rolling terrain and wooded areas on the hilltops. It was spoilt to a degree by the number of advertisements on the sides of the roads. On arrival at the farm, we were greeted by Bill's wife, Auntie Bernice, their only son Billy and five girl cousins, Lillian, Dorothy, Phyllis, Margery, and Caroline. They had all turned out to welcome their English cousin and I found it quite embarrassing being the centre of attraction.

This was the start of a great adventure and I was fortunate in being able to work side-by-side with a man who had very thorough experience of all facets of farming. He had about fifty Holstein milking cows and used Surge milking machines which were suspended on straps over the animals with an adjustment that enabled the weight of the container to be increased during the milking process. The milk was eventually put into churns which were then put into an underground cooler filled with water. Uncle Bill's next door neighbour, Harry Dunlap, would help when grass cutting started and I always remember his famous shout when things got difficult, 'Hen Turkey'. When the milk lorry arrived these churns were hauled out of the cooler and thrown on to the back of the truck. I was used to handling ten-gallon churns, imperial gallons at that, whilst unknown to me these were eight-gallon churns (American) and much lighter. The British churns would weigh about 130 lbs whereas the American was only about 90 lbs. Unfortunately, in showing off how strong I was and not realising this difference in weight I gave a tremendous heave and threw the churn so hard that the lid came off and the milk went all over the lorry bed. Not an encouraging start.

This was very much a country area and there was not a lot of entertainment locally. We did get to the bowling alley and I became proficient in American ten-pin bowling based on the original English game, but now all automatic.

My eldest cousin Lillian, named after my mother, was married to Roy Gregrow and they had a farm not far away. On one day, my uncle asked me to take a horse to them which involved a journey of some miles through a German immigrant community where there was a bridge with loose wooden slats. This time I had a saddle, but the horse baulked at the unstable base to the bridge and after several attempts I had to get off and walk it over the bridge. A popular pastime in the area was shooting woodchucks, ('How much wood could a woodchuck chuck if a wood chuck could chuck wood?'), indigenous to the USA and like a mole. On another occasion I spotted a bird on a cable at the side of the farmhouse and shot at it with a rifle. Unfortunately, I missed the bird but hit the cable and the television aerial collapsed on the roof of the house to the chagrin of Uncle Bill.

The Needham Farmhouse, originally 1840, Homestead

The grass-cutting season was fast approaching, but first it was necessary to prepare the silo and auger, etc. My uncle had two silos, one was a modern metal one and the other was an original wooden one with steel straps around the circumference which had to be tightened before the new grass was put into it. They were both sixty feet high and the wooden one had a ladder attached to the side. My uncle sent me up this to tighten the straps with a spanner. Fortunately, I never had any difficulty with heights and the job was completed satisfactorily although if my mother had known she would have had a heart attack! The transportable auger was set against the silo and had a trough which was filled with new grass from the moving bed of the trailer and a drum of molasses was

Needham farm silos. The original wooden silo on the left

attached to the fan end which blew the grass and the molasses into the silo. In due course, this mixture gave a sweet smelling feed for the cattle in contrast to the bitter (butyric acid) silage produced in the UK in pit silos. Beforehand, however, my uncle had decided that we needed a new bulk grass-carrying trailer and we went out into the woods and chopped down the trees required. These were then pulled to a local sawmill with a tractor which sawed them into planks. We used the old axles and the trailer was built from scratch with a moving floor.

My uncle had decided previously that he must have a new forage harvester. This is towed by the tractor and cuts the grass and blows it into the trailer following behind. Prior to my visit local farmers in the area had got together with the distributors and it was arranged that their products would be displayed working in a field side-by-side when the prospective customers would make their choice. This was a typical American arrangement, the winner takes all. There were several makes including John Deere, Massey-Harris, etc., but my uncle chose to buy a little known make called the Fox, as it turned out to be the most efficient. We therefore started cutting the grass with the new forage harvester using two trailers. When one was full, we would change to the other tractor and take it down to the silo, unload it into the auger and blow it into the silo. It was during this period that we were asked to do another farmer's crop and I particularly remember going with my uncle who drove the large Case tractor (the only chain-driven tractor in the world) towing the forage harvester and myself driving the Ferguson tractor pulling the auger. This was at the time that there was a dispute

Above: *The Fox forage harvester, Americans call them "choppers"*

Left: *Case tractor with chain drive. The manufacturer claims they never had a chain break!*

between Harry Ferguson and Henry Ford over the design of the light tractor. They were both painted grey, but Ford had a red badge and Ferguson a blue one. History shows that Ferguson was to win the dispute and received millions in damages, but nowadays the Ford vehicle badges are always on a blue background. Did Henry Ford insist he had the blue badge in compensation?

We duly arrived at our neighbour's and cut his mixture of grass and beans and filled his silo. My uncle told me to get off and return to the farm with the auger and it was on this journey that I forgot, with it being a central steering wheel position, that I should be driving on the right hand side of the road. Fortunately, on this quiet country road, I only met one car, which approached at quite a fast speed and only at the last minute was I able to swerve to the other side and so avoid a head on accident. My only pathetic reply to the driver's angry outburst was to explain in my best 'Toff's' English accent that we usually drove on the other side of the road!

Ron with Dorothy, the most attentive of all my American cousins

My uncle had a new Buick Dynaflow car and occasionally I would take this for a run on the back roads with my cousin Dorothy. I did not have an American driving licence, but it did not seem to matter in this country area. It was on one of these trips that I did a hundred miles per hour for the first time. The Dynaflow was one of the first automatic gearboxes and the power loss was quite apparent when accelerating with the feeling of a slipping clutch. It was a very comfortable car, but along these second class country roads, it was like a ship in a rough sea, especially at speed.

During the period I was in the USA, my uncle did not pay me any wages although a figure had been agreed. I just asked him now and again for some money which must have accumulated over a period. Eventually the time came to return home and my uncle and I returned to New York City to catch the *Queen Mary* for Southampton. We went a few days before the ship was due to sail and went sightseeing, mainly going to different theatre shows, including the Rockettes in Radio City, the largest high kick dancing group in the world, ascending the Chrysler Building (then the highest skyscraper in the world) which had previously been hit by an aircraft and part of the viewing platform was roped off where it was damaged. On another occasion, we went down to the bowery in New York, and although we did not stay at any particular nightclub, I recollect Gene Krupa playing the drums on a visit there. I also took the opportunity to buy presents for my family after my uncle had handed over the balance of my wages. These were to cost even more in import duty than the purchase price when I went through customs at Southampton.

Fast return journey to the UK (5 days), "Cheers"

The return journey was very eventful again, because there were many young people travelling to universities in the UK, and one particularly attractive and vivacious American female called Helen Guggenheim. All the young men gathered round her like 'moths round a flame' including myself. Before we left the ship at Southampton, we swapped addresses.

My uncle Victor, my mother's youngest brother, collected me at Southampton, and paid the import tax due. Some time later, in 1951, when I was staying at his house in Bournemouth, his daughter, my cousin Hazel and I travelled by car to the Festival of Britain exhibition in London and called at Helen Guggenheim's address, only to be told that she was away on her honeymoon with Sir Keith Joseph (later to become a minister in Mrs Thatcher's government).

I had learnt a considerable amount about farming from my uncle Billy and his wife Bernice looked after me as though I was one of their own. He was to die in 1994 while she lived to 2005 to the grand old age of 101 years. On my return, I was still eighteen years old, and National Service was obligatory for eighteen-year-olds at the time, but those in the reserved occupations were exempt. Farming was a reserved occupation and therefore if I continued farming, I would not have to do National Service.

However, I had always been interested in British military history and would have preferred to have gone into an infantry regiment, but realised that this was not an option because of my 'gammy' leg. After the period as an apprentice mechanic at Davenport Garage and my interest in motorsport, it seemed an opportunity to see if I could further my mechanical knowledge and applied for the REME. Unfortunately, I failed the aptitude test and I was offered a position in the RAOC instead. I passed the medical because I never mentioned the problem with my 'gammy' leg.

I was sent to Aldershot for basic training and I arrived at Salamanca Barracks on the 1st of September 1949. The military discipline at Salamanca was ridiculous. They had a system which tried to 'belittle' the recruit. An example of this was bed inspection which if unsatisfactory, instead of asking the recruit to do it again, suggested that all the bed clothes were thrown at the ceiling! This was conducted by corporals and after having had a spell at boarding school, I found it very irritating. Clearly it was intended to frighten new recruits,

Ron at Salamanca Barracks in Aldershot - Ready for anything!, October 1949

but it had the opposite effect on me. A regiment of airborne engineers were in the next barracks and I was very tempted at one point to volunteer to serve with them.

At the end of this basic training period, I was sent to the transport depot at Chilwell in Nottinghamshire. Although I had taken part in all activities up to this point, I was beginning to feel frustration at the pointlessness of army service in peace time, but also because there were signs that my 'gammy' leg was not going to stand up to all the marching, etc. The only good thing I could see about the army in peacetime appeared to be the organised sports and although I could not take part in team games, I enjoyed the gymnasium with weight lifting, etc. However, whilst at Chilwell, my leg deteriorated further and after seeing the MO I was excused parades with the diagnosis of a 'mobile cartilage'. Soon after this there was a regimental parade at the depot for a visiting general, and the RSM, a six-foot six-inch Scots Guardsman, organised the same. At one end of the parade ground which the regiment faced, there was a row of trees with a spotlight in each of the tree branches. During the parade and the presentation of arms with rifles the lights would flash which was the sign to every soldier to react to the standard drill procedure. The whole regiment on parade appeared to be so well trained that they could have been a regiment of guardsmen. Whether the general knew about this subterfuge, I never knew.

Meanwhile, before the arrival of the general and his staff I was being excused parades, but had to stand on the sideline. It wasn't long before the RSM noticed me and waved to me to come over to speak to him. I therefore proceeded to march with the best 'limp' I could pretend and when I arrived in front of him, he asked me, 'Why are you not on parade laddie?'

I replied, 'Because I have a mobile cartilage.'

He gave me a withering look and then said, 'That's the only bloody thing that's mobile about you, clear off.'

The 17/21st Lancers (Death's Head) were at this depot with their Centurion tanks and we were, of course, expected to service them. One of the corporals in our company was an exceptional mechanic and had a trick with a running Bedford petrol-engine lorry of getting hold of a spark plug with one hand and holding a penny with the other and made the spark jump from the penny to the wing of the lorry. Quite spectacular, but I had been shown by my uncle Bill in America how to hold on to an electric fence and use the intermittent electric shock to surprise casual bystanders, particularly the girls at agricultural college.

By this time, I was fed up with the army and with my inability to take part in sport that I asked to be discharged. I went for a medical and on my telling them that I would not claim a pension, I was discharged on the 27th of February 1950. However, there was one beneficial effect of my short-lived army service which was the discipline ingrained with regard to guns. Always very strict on the handling of same, I was given a Bren machine-gun, probably because I was strong enough to carry it, but also because I had shown a very speedy aptitude in changing the gas cylinder to prevent the barrel over heating in continuous firing. This in-built training was to avoid a tragic accident explained later when on holiday in Florida.

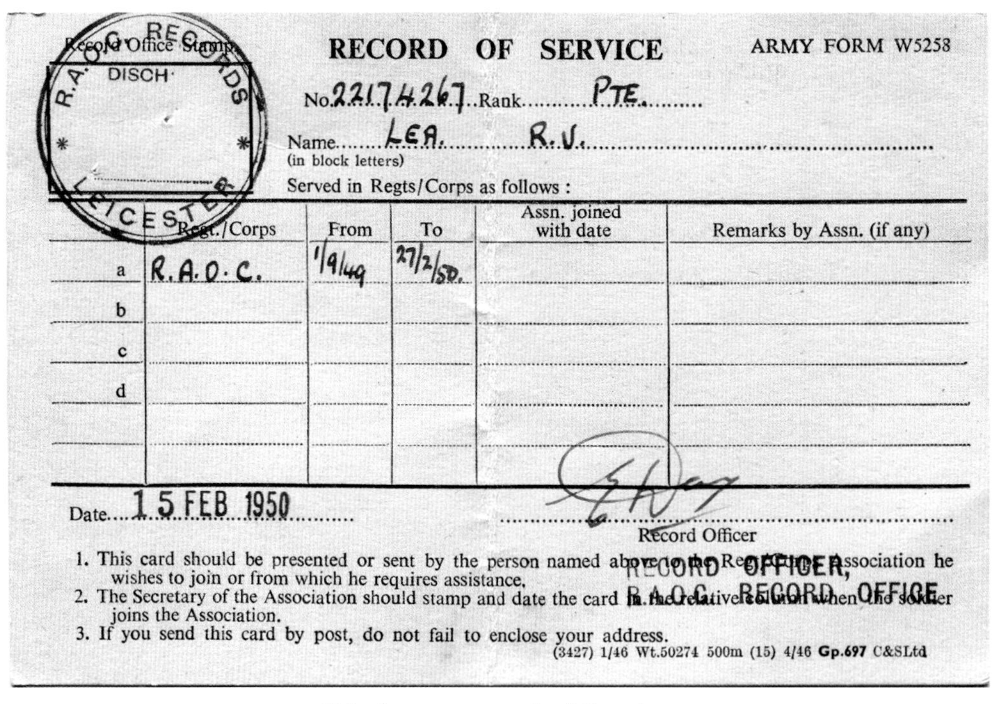

Record Office Stamp: R.A.O.C. RECORDS LEICESTER DISCH.

RECORD OF SERVICE

ARMY FORM W5258

No. 22174267 Rank PTE.

Name LEA. R.V.
(in block letters)

Served in Regts/Corps as follows :

	Regt./Corps	From	To	Assn. joined with date	Remarks by Assn. (if any)
a	R.A.O.C.	1/9/49	27/2/50		
b					
c					
d					

Date 15 FEB 1950

Record Officer
RECORD OFFICER, R.A.O.C. RECORD OFFICE

1. This card should be presented or sent by the person named above to the Regimental Association he wishes to join or from which he requires assistance.
2. The Secretary of the Association should stamp and date the card in the relative column when the soldier joins the Association.
3. If you send this card by post, do not fail to enclose your address.

(3427) 1/46 Wt.50274 500m (15) 4/46 **Gp.697** C&SLtd

Discharge record of Service

CHAPTER 4

A Beneficial Learning Experience

I had now decided I would like to go to agricultural college because being with my Uncle Bill in America, I had learned much more about farming and found out it was not just about labouring. The diploma course at the Cheshire School of Agriculture, Reaseheath, Nantwich, was for nine months and was co-educational. The girls did all the milking of the two herds, one Friesian and the other Ayrshire, at the Home Farm. The boys did other agricultural work in between lectures in the school classrooms.

We were treated quite differently to pupils at school and were looked upon as mature students and, in fact, there were some who were quite a bit older than myself. However, although I could not play active sport, my reputation had arrived ahead of me and I was made non-playing Captain of the school football team. It was one of the most pleasant periods of my life and one I enjoyed, not only because of the new-found responsibility, but also because of the freedom of being able to study something I was really interested in.

By this time I was able to afford my first car, which was an Austin 7 soft top and occasionally I used it to come home at the weekends. The principal of the college was a Mr Lamberton, a dour Scot, and the vice-principal was Mr Shuttleworth who had the regular duty of going round the farm buildings and barns at night to check that these very virile male and female students were not cohabiting out of hours. One of Mr Lamberton's famous comments was words to the effect that it was a good job it was no more than a nine months' course, otherwise the college population would have increased substantially!

The girls were under the control of Mrs Benyon, a well known figure in the Cheshire dairy industry, and she and all the girls lived in a separate residence adjacent to the college. On one occasion, we male students decided to raid the residence and it was found out that Mrs Benyon and her assistant had bedrooms opposite each other and some of the boys crept in late at night and tied a rope between the two inward-opening doors. However, they had not taken into account that there was a temporary student lecturer in residence, and eventually she was to undo the rope, allowing Mrs Benyon and her assistant out of their bedrooms.

Cheshire School of Agriculture, Reaseheath, Nantwich. Full complement of staff and students at the end of the course, 1950. Ron fourth row, 5th from right

At this point, there was much panic amongst the intruders as it was almost certain that any boy caught in the residence at night would have been expelled. I recollect getting into the wardrobe in one of the girls' bedrooms but, unfortunately, the wardrobe did not have a handle on the inside and I could not hold it closed. Therefore, I vacated the wardrobe and went to the washrooms and saw the key for the emergency fire escape in a box with a glass front on the wall. Wrapping a towel around my hand, I broke the glass and took the key and went to the external stairway of the fire escape and managed to get away with the cheers of my co-conspirators ringing in my ears. I was the last to get out of the building.

It was on another occasion in the common room between lectures and reading *Motorcycle News* that I read about the practice times for the Tourist Trophy Race in the Isle of Man and this was of great interest to several students, including one who lived on the Isle of Man, where his mother had a boarding house in Douglas. He had a 650cc BSA Gold Star motorcycle which he kept in a barn on a local farm. The forthcoming Saturday, all the students were due to visit the Cheshire Agricultural Show and my Manx friend and I began to discuss the possibilities of being able to get time off to go to see the senior TT on the Friday. The warden was a Mr Moss and although we did not hold out much hope for his agreement, we decided that if we could leave the college on the Thursday night, we could catch the ferry in time. To our surprise, he agreed as long as we returned by the Sunday evening. In great excitement, therefore, we went down to the barn and raced over to Liverpool to get the Thursday midnight boat to Douglas and arrived there in the early hours of the morning. We then travelled up to his mother's boarding house and had a super breakfast before setting out to watch the race. Being a native of the island, my friend knew all the back ways to the different corners and we were able to watch this memorable race at several of the most exciting points. I was to visit the Isle of Man TT races later, but this was certainly the most memorable because of the last minute arrangements and the special circumstances of being able to see Geoff Duke win the senior TT on a 500cc Norton motorcycle.

After a most enjoyable nine months at the end of which I received a diploma and before the final exams, I put an advertisement in the *Farmers Weekly* newspaper in which I stated I had six months' experience of American grassland farming. This advertisement received several replies, one in particular from an American who had been born in the UK and in his retirement had returned to farm in Wales. It was a letter that expressed the hopes of an elderly retired man who had no son and in effect stating that if I was the right person the farm would be left to me in due course. The letter arrived during the final examinations and unfortunately, because of this I did not reply immediately. In retrospect the offer was so generous that I should have immediately gone down to meet him and confirm my interest. When I eventually wrote it was some time before I had a reply and then it was from his secretary who basically said the offer had been withdrawn. This was a once in a lifetime opportunity which I have always regretted missing.

Another reply was from a farmer in Mickle Trafford near Chester and I went to meet him and accepted the job which was as a manager at the time, employing two experienced workers with a dairy herd and some poultry. I lived in the farmhouse with his wife and two children. They had one draught horse, but I had no real experience of working horses. I recollect that on one occasion I was asked to bring the horse out, and instead of handling it by the forelock which was the usual way when there was no head harness attached, I grabbed it by the ear which the horse did not appreciate and took off round the farmyard with me hanging on for dear life! I was not asked to get the horse out again.

At this time, there was a good market for pigs and as the hens were in battery cages and not doing very well, I persuaded the farmer to buy some pigs. We started in a small way and when the pigs had reached the required weight, we did not have a proper scale and I tried to weigh them on a Salters balance in a sack. Obviously this was a very haphazard method because the pigs hardly stopped jumping and I had to practically throttle them to keep them still.

I kept my Austin 7 at the farm, and on some weekends would return home in it and whilst left at the front of my parents house, a mutual friend of my brother and myself, Guy Entwistle, used a stencil to print on the bonnet of my car 'LOT 69'. Although I had the technical knowledge, I did not really have the practical experience to be the manager of this farm and my mother suggested that I should join the family firm where my brother was already working, and I gave my notice to the farmer and left.

First car, Austin 7 Tourer with latest air conditioning system!

It was in February 1952 that I went to the Manchester University Students' Rag Ball held in the Whitworth Hall. There was a tradition for the students to collect money for charity on Shrove Tuesday, culminating in them having a 'free-for-all' dance where everybody and anything goes. I went in my most 'sartorial gear', a tee-shirt and jeans with a bottle of rum in my back pocket and wearing a straw panama hat! It was not long before I noticed two girls, and one of these was particularly interesting. Having introduced myself in spite of my rough appearance, it turned out they were sisters, Sheila and Julie Slater, and the former was to become my wife. The Slater family lived in Poynton, Cheshire, and after making contact at the Rag Ball, I would cycle to Poynton to see my new girlfriend.

It was on these journeys that I would often see a strange 'bat-like' figure hovering in the sky. A menacing sight which I learnt later was the new delta-wing aircraft manufactured at A. V. Roe at Woodford, the Avro Vulcan. Some years later when sales manager of the family company in Manchester, Joseph Lea & Sons Ltd, I received a phone call from the experimental department at A. V. Roe with a request that I should call on them. No details were given but when I arrived I was warned that secrecy was of vital national importance before I was taken into the inner sanctum and shown the drawings of the Blue Streak missile. They required a trailer to carry this formidable armament for loading into the Vulcan. This was at the height of the Cold War and the intention was for the Vulcan to launch the missile before the Russian border towards Moscow. In fact, the Blue Streak was far too large for the Leason works capacity and in any event the Cold War was to 'thaw' soon after.

CHAPTER 5

Clogs to Clogs in Three Generations

My great-grandfather Joseph Lea had been a foreman turner at W. E. Cary at Red Bank, Manchester, founded in 1848, and twenty-one years later he went up the road to Dyche Street and started his own company as a manufacturer of road springs, iron bodywork, steel stockholders and wholesaler of all wheelwright requirements including artillery wheels and coach pattern wheels. He had two sons, John my grandfather and Peter his brother. John had three sons, Joseph, Harry my father and Geoffrey. However, Peter only had two daughters and there was a company rule which prevented girls from working in and becoming owners of the company. Although this prevented a fragmentation of ownership, it was clearly unfair and could not be defended in modern times. Joseph had two daughters, Joan and Barbara, and Geoffrey the youngest brother one daughter, Brenda. Only my father had sons – Peter and myself – and one daughter, Christine, and we were therefore in the advantageous position of being the future owners, but in fact this never happened.

Close coupled 4 wheel trailer outside Joseph Lea & Sons Ltd in Manchester

I started work at the company at the end of 1951 as the company's sales representative. I had to use my own car, a Peugeot 203 which was only 1204 cc, but which had excellent road-holding and very accurate steering. I first had a period of training in all the aspects of spring-making and repairs, wheelwright products and trailer and caravan accessories.

There was a comprehensive wheelwright catalogue prepared by my grandfather John Lea and a very fine illustrated caravan equipment catalogue which my father

Trailer Tent designed by Harry Lea and made in the Leason factory, 1923

Harry Lea with a 2 wheel flat bed trailer outside the works where it was made, 1936

had produced under the trade name Leason, which became the first and principal supplier of caravan equipment in the country, originally all by mail order, whereby it was known as the 'Caravanners' Encyclopaedia'. My father designed a camping trailer in 1923 and introduced all the caravan accessories which were sold by mail order.

It was not long before I was sent out to call on customers in both the wheelwright trade and the caravan trade. Although the caravan equipment business had been founded by my father it was mostly retail and I was intent on developing it with the trade. Some caravan dealers such as Ken Montrose of Montrose Caravans of Cheadle, Cheshire were not interested in stocking and supplying caravan accessories because as he said it took as much time to sell accessories as it did to sell caravans, and there was such a great difference in profit. However, the majority of dealers thought otherwise as their caravan customers preferred to be able to view and inspect any additional equipment they required.

After the war, a new caravan equipment company was set up by two ex-RAF personnel, Ernie King and Bernard Joy, Joy & King Limited. Their big advantage was that they were in London and had an extensive shop, so that they did not rely on mail order to the same extent. I got to know Ernie King later when he told me that when they started their company, because Leasons were so well known, he visited Manchester and, in disguise with a false moustache, called at the small shop in Dyche Street to see how his main competitor organised things. When I had my own company later, he would call at our show stand in the Earls Court Caravan Exhibition, and we would discuss these early days.

Originally, therefore, having covered all facets of the business, I would call on customers in both the wheelwright and caravan trade. One of the most interesting characters in the wheelwright business, called John Fishwick, was the only one I ever met who knew my-great grandfather Joseph Lea, the founder of the company, as a young boy. He told me he was dapper little man, always correctly dressed, and made it his business to go out and meet customers although he was a practical qualified engineer. He must have realised that future success would only come about by going out and drumming up business. Perhaps some of these genes were passed on to me.

Other interesting characters were in Liverpool and these people had a particularly dry humour. I remember one telling me the story about a man who had died 'in flagrante delicto'. Many of these wheelwrights were also funeral directors and on putting the body into the coffin they could not close the coffin lid because of the protuberance stopping same. The wheelwright funeral director and his assistant therefore sat back to consider the next step. In the end it was decided that they would drill a hole in the lid so that the protuberance could pass through and they would plane it off so that it looked like a knot in the wood! Another suggestion was that a bouquet of flowers should be arranged to hide the protuberance. It was this sort of dry humour that they were famous for and made my visits very entertaining.

Although I was not a trained engineer like my brother who served time as an apprentice with Reynold Chains, I had to become familiar with the manufacturing works. The staff there included two blacksmiths, Mick and Bob, ex-railwaymen from Derby, also strikers and furnacemen and spring forgers, etc. Prior to Bob joining the company there was another Irishman working there called Matt Hammersley, an appropriate name for a blacksmith. He was, however, a bad-tempered type apparently and very often chased his striker round the floor with his hammer because he had struck the steel inappropriately! Loads of coke and coal were kept outside for the furnaces and it was known that at weekends some was stolen by the people in the cottages opposite. However, they made sure no outsiders did this so it was worth the small losses.

I was beginning to build up a clientele of trade customers in the caravan industry and one of these was Jim Swallow of Willerby Units, Heywood, Lancashire. Jim was a great character with a broad Lancashire accent. In fact he could speak in such a broad Lancashire dialect that it sounded like a foreign language. He was full of his own 'home truths' such as 'always marry a girl socially well below you because then she will always be grateful for everything you give her'.

Willerby Caravans were at Willerby, near Hull, and one of the first caravan manufacturers in the country. In fact, they were originally makers of beehives known as Yorkshire Apiaries who were to have their first chassis in 1948 from Leason. However, they lost the business some time previously when Jim Swallow came up with a simple design of a reinforced chassis which Willerby Caravans thought would give them an advantage over their competitors. Originally, a caravan chassis was designed to be rigid only when the body framing had been completed and otherwise was very flexible. However, Jim's design had a cantilever reinforcement underneath like a bridge and was very rigid even without the body. He was interested in buying all the parts for these chassis including couplings, jockey wheels, brace legs and axles. I was unable to get the order for axles, but persuaded him to buy the couplings, jockey wheels and brace legs from ourselves. This was never straightforward as there was a lot of competition, but the main competitor lost their chance of business when Jim found out that they had quoted him a price which he accepted and then delivered the goods and invoiced him at a higher price. It was only when pushing

Ron on holiday on the beach at Paignton, Devon

Paignton holiday friends: Val Withington, Doug Wallace, Margaret Tinker, Peter Withington and Sheila. All were to marry later.

for sales and giving him prices that he looked at the invoices and found he had been overcharged by this other company. From then on he placed his business with Leason because he know we would never try to 'fiddle' him. The orders were now quite considerable and he was making over 100 chassis per week for Willerby Caravans. He was a great publicist and borrowed elephants from Billy Smart's Circus and had one stand on the chassis and photographed it to show its inherent strength.

By this time we had become friends and he agreed to loan me his Wolseley 6/90 saloon car to go on holiday with friends in Devon. Another good customer, Stan Woodliffe of Woodliffe Caravan Agency in Paignton, Devon, had agreed to loan two of his static caravans for a week's holiday. We were three couples, not married, but all courting which was why we had to have the two caravans. It seems that these days this would not have been necessary, we would have all mixed in together, but at the time it was not usual to sleep with your girlfriend. It was a very good holiday and we had some great fun. This example of the friendship I developed with certain customers was based on trust and was a criteria I followed throughout my business life.

Ready to leave the Woodliffe Caravan Park in the 6/90 Wolseley saloon

My father had designed with a local engineer in Rochdale, J. W. Taylor, a quick detachable (QD) coupling which had a reputation of reliability and safety. The only disadvantage was that it had to be locked when on the ball peg by hand. This left the possibility of human error in not locking on to the ball and other competitors, particularly B & B, introduced a coupling which was self-locking. The only tourer caravan manufacturer who made his own chassis to buy the Leason QD coupling was Holgate Caravans of Tintwistle, Lancashire, and this was a particular advantage for practical testing for its performance and reliability, regarding which the owner, Arthur Holgate, was constantly in touch. It was particularly significant that much later my brother designed a self-locking coupling based on the QD principle called the Lockmatic, but because we had no practical trade users early problems could not be eradicated quickly. This new design had come about after J. W. Taylor could not keep up with the production of the QD coupling to meet the orders I had received, and it was decided that the new coupling should be introduced and would be made in-house.

My sales philosophy was to build up a sense of complete reliability so that the makers of caravans, trailers or chassis could be absolutely certain that their production would not be held up for the lack of equipment. Customers could only develop this confidence through experience and therefore it was necessary to obtain the business in the first place. This sometimes meant offering prices which initially could not be justified by the quantity ordered.

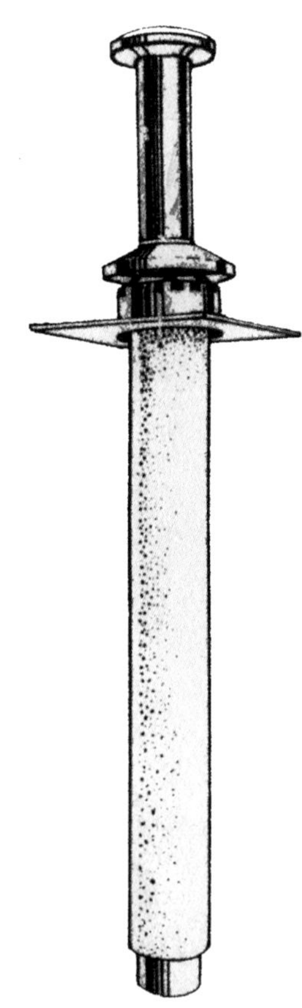

Combined flue assembly for Holiday Caravans and Mobile Homes

An example of this was the combined flue assembly used by the static holiday caravan manufacturers. In the fifties all static holiday caravans had small solid fuel stoves either the Torgem, Sylvan or Artayco. They all had to have flue assemblies with cast iron inner pipes and six-inch asbestos outer pipes which were assembled with clamps in their factories. Following a visit to Nene Valley Coachworks in Rushden, Northamptonshire, who were one of the largest manufacturers and whose senior staff, Roy Cattell and Stuart Freeman, co-managing directors, Jack Goodliffe, works director and Barry Bentley, sales director, had all become good friends and very good customers, I proposed to them that to save labour we could assemble the flue assemblies and deliver them complete to the length required. The basis of this, which became known as a combined flue assembly, was a four-inch cast iron pipe with a six-inch asbestos outer pipe cut to the length required and the two pipes held together with hardened self-tapping screws.

This assembly I developed became recognised by the British Standards, BS3212, Code of Practice 340, but in order to compete with the material prices the manufacturers were paying it was necessary to work to a very low profit margin, i.e. 15% to start with which later became much greater, i.e. 60%, when the quantities increased. They also had to have the confidence that we would never let them down with delivery and so hold up the production line. They soon found out that they could rely on delivery and stocking ahead was not necessary so that the system of 'just in time' method of supply was accepted.

Meanwhile, the spring repair and ironworks side of the business was just ticking over and losing money as was the retail and mail order side of the caravan business. We had now started to take a stand at the Caravan Exhibition at Earls Court and this was my responsibility. Although this was an opportunity for publicity for retail and trade sales, being in the north of England the former was quickly becoming irrelevant even though we had a caravan equipment shop at the Leason business address.

One caravan distributor in particular, W. D. Harrington of Delamere, Cheshire, who were on the main route for caravanners visiting North Wales for weekends or longer holidays, had developed their caravan accessory department substantially which made a tortuous journey into Manchester with its increasing traffic much less desirable, and at one point it was considered whether we should move our business out into a similar area, but in the end at my suggestion we formed a depot in Dunstable, Bedfordshire, to take advantage of the increasing trade in the south of England. Before this, however, in an effort to increase the trade with caravan distributors and caravan parts stockists we commissioned a mobile caravan showroom initially to be pulled by a Land Rover. We employed a representative, Eric Cavanagh, who towed this unit all over the country, and it was well received by customers. It was fitted out comprehensively with all the goods we sold including solid fuel stoves, sink units, toilet units, etc. and weighed about two and a half tons, but the Land Rover did not have the power. It was, therefore, replaced with a standard Vanguard van which with its very strong 4-cylinder 2-litre engine, was able to cope with this excessive weight. However, after this first season when customers were enthusiastic and quick to take time to look round the mobile showroom it became a bit of a liability after they had seen the contents several times and were not prepared to go out of their way.

Mobile Showroom with 2 litre Standard Vanguard van outside retail shop

Ron proves that a Sales Manager's job is not just about getting orders, but demands some elbow grease as well

The business connections which had been developed by this system of taking our caravan accessories showroom to their premises made the potential of a shop in the south of England more viable and a depot was developed. Eric Cavanagh, the manager of the shop in Dunstable, was able to visit customers in the south regularly. I was now the sales manager and had the job of supervising the development of this expansion, the caravan accessory business with the trade was at least 80% of the turnover. In addition, I was calling on caravan distributors with shops, caravan parks and independent caravan shops from Scotland, both the east and west coasts of England and occasionally the south coast. Except for a few loyal customers, I found these retail outlets of caravan accessories were very fickle and it became more and more a case of first come, first served. The sales representatives who called first in the week would get the bulk of the order for replacement goods, with the result that representatives of different companies were always trying to get in front of the competition by changing their schedule.

In view of this, I started to concentrate on the manufacturers, both tourer, static holiday and mobile homes. Most of my competitors believed that it was not possible to sell equipment to the caravan manufacturers because of their bulk buying and generally dealing direct with the equipment manufacturers. However, I realised that it was not just about price, because they had a production schedule which if interrupted by a lack of supplies would badly affect their turnover. To the touring caravan manufacturers, I sold electric cable, seven-inch plugs and sockets (imported from Wilhelm Harting in Germany), fibreglass towbar gas bottle cabinets, electric water pumps and stainless steel sink and drainer units, etc. Initially, all tourer manufacturers fitted plastic sink and drainer units, but I persuaded Terry Read, the boss of Ace Caravans Limited, to fit a twenty-eight-by-fourteen-inch stainless steel unit which was the first time such a long-life unit had been fitted as original equipment in a mass-produced touring caravan.

The Leason stand at the Earls Court Caravan Exhibition displaying a range of caravan equipment including the Artayco stove with a static holiday caravan flue assembly and flue heated water tank / roof cowl to BS3212 CP340

All the manufacturers had trade shows at the end of the year to show the distributors and park owners their new range for the following year. I attended most of them, but one particular show I attended was at Cresta Caravans of Hull where one of their main distributors, Frank Panter (brother of Charles Panter, the boss of manufacturer Berkeley Caravans and later the maker of the little three-wheeler car) asked if they could fit a black perspex sink and drainer unit in the touring caravans he wished to order for next season. The boss of Cresta asked me if this was possible. Nobody had ever heard of a black sink and drainer unit and it would hardly be practical in view of the scurvy associated with the washing of pans and crockery, so I said they were unlikely to be available. He then asked a representative of a competitor present if they would be able to supply. He replied in the affirmative. When I heard this, I telephoned the sink unit maker P & S Plastics of Love Lane Estate, Cirencester,

INCORPORATED
SALES MANAGERS'
ASSOCIATION

This is to Certify that R.V. Lea
has this day been elected an Associate of the Association *Dated* 15th January *1959*

President *Chairman*

Director ~~*and Secretary*~~

Sales Managers' Association

and asked them if they could make a black plastic sink and drainer which they confirmed they could. I instructed them to make a sample and despatch it direct by passenger train to Cresta Caravans of Hull. I then returned to the showroom and told the boss of Cresta that a sample black unit was on the way to them, on which news they ordered fifty units for the touring caravans Frank Panter had ordered. This is an example of how in sales one must always be alive to the 'avant garde' request even though you know it is not practical.

During this period the biggest development was in regard to the heating of mobile homes. We were already supplying flue assemblies to both the static holiday and mobile home makers, particularly Omar Mobile Homes of Thetford, Norfolk, which incorporated a five-inch diameter cast iron pipe with a seven-inch asbestos outer pipe. The two pipes held together in the same way as the static holiday caravan system. In this case the inner cast iron pipe was wrapped with glass wool because much larger solid fuel stoves were fitted in these bigger units and it gave extra fireproof security. On test at Omar our larger combined assembly had a much lower temperature on the outside compared to the stainless steel unit usually fitted domestically and industrially and the only alternative in the BS3212.

Although traditional and giving a low condensation, the solid fuel appliance fitted in the UK for central heating by radiator and hot water was in contrast to the method used in the USA, where for some years they had fitted blown air units fired by gas or oil, which helped to reduce condensation by means of the movement of air which could provide air conditioning (which was a long way off fifty years ago), I believed it would be possible to incorporate a pressure jet oil or gas fired (Calor Gas) boiler which would provide central heating and hot water in the traditional way, but with automatic control and without the dust and dirt of storage problems with solid fuel. I therefore contacted Mr T. A. Atkinson, the boss of Perkins Boilers of Derby and between us we designed a compact unit incorporating one of their 60,000 BTU pressure jet boilers within an angle steel frame containing a Primatic (combined central heating and hot water) tank above the boiler complete with an accelerator pump and all the electrics including fuses. This was aimed at the mobile home makers and Omar Homes of Thetford particularly. Mr Atkinson and myself travelled down to Thetford when the new system was presented to them. However, it was Lisset Mobile Homes in East Yorkshire who were the first to order this innovative new unit. This company was owned by a Mr Wheelhouse, a most appropriate name for a mobile home manufacturer and one of the most forward thinking in the industry.

Perkins Boilers of Derby were an old established company and it was one of the sons of the founder who had gone to the USA to see the high speed diesel engines and returned to found Perkins Diesels of Peterborough. After the design of the composite unit had been finalised it was necessary for me to go to the factory in Derby and learn something about pressure jet gas boilers. This was a one-to-one instruction by Mr Atkinson's son. Although the new unit was profitable it did not receive the immediate support of other mobile home makers, probably because it was so much more money than the simple solid fuel stove with its back boiler and separate water cylinder. However, we had a 'foot in both camps' so it was not of immediate concern and I realised it would take time to become established. I had now developed the wholesale side of the business so that it was the mainstay with the retail and engineering side being very small in comparison and the spring manufacturing side, which was practically finished.

However, I still found time to call on Sam Longson at Chapel-en-le-Frith (where I was to live later), who dropped off their commercial road springs with their own transport each week and collected it when finished, typically the only regular customer we had for this department. In addition to the manufacturers of tourer, static and mobile homes, there were other specialised makers of industrial units that we dealt with. One of these was Mobac Joinery of Garstang who built towable units for hire to building and construction companies on site. We had a good relationship with the manager because he appreciated we would never let him down with lack of supplies, so we automatically received all his orders for fittings and equipment. On one occasion I even took urgent requirements in my small car to make sure production was not held up.

Therefore, whilst the wholesale side was developing very well, the drain on the company finances of the original spring making/repair side, the archaic wheelwright side and not least the director's salary to my Uncle Joe, who was in charge of this side of the business, was to result in the demise of this long-established company. Only my brother's engineering/trailer department and the retail shop side were breaking even. In my opinion the fact that my father's brothers only had daughters affected their attitudes in developing the business for the future. As no female descendants could inherit ownership they were content in obtaining a good living in their own lifetime.

My father was often in confrontation with his eldest brother Joe who was a workaholic, very accurate in everything he did but without initiative or imagination. Unfortunately, through their strict upbringing my father was never able to challenge his older brother that change was absolutely necessary if the company was to survive. My father's younger brother Geoffrey Lea had died in 1956 and he clearly used the fraught relationship between his two older brothers to 'feather' his nest with the minimum attendance at the office even though he was a practical and very intelligent man. Uncle Joe's two daughters, Joan and Barbara, were educated intelligent people who were to hold responsible positions, Joan the agent of the Conservative Party in Manchester and the Lady Mayoress to her husband Victor Guthrie when elected Mayor of Bury, and Barbara the Registrar of Birth, Deaths and Marriages also in Bury. It was the expressed opinion of my cousin Joan Guthrie that the 'curse' in the relationship between the third generation brothers was due to the divisive upbringing by their mother. These very able female cousins would have been an asset if employed by Joseph Lea & Sons Ltd as managers if the rules had allowed it but whether their input could have made the business more viable and saved it from liquidation is open to question. Perhaps 'too many cooks spoil the broth'.

In February 1964 I wrote to Uncle Joe a very diplomatic letter expressing concern for his recent illness which prevented him attending the office, but pointing out he was well past retirement age (over seventy years) and that the responsibility for the success of the firm now rested with my brother Peter and myself, for which we should receive commensurate directors' salaries. I also pointed out that we both had substantial mortgages whereas both he and his brothers were given their homes by their father, John Lea, and that we were paying expensive endowment insurance so that we could retire at the normal pension age of sixty-five years. This letter caused a big row within the family, but nothing changed.

Earlier in 1964 when attending a motor race at Silverstone with my friend Alex Bullen and in the inevitable traffic queue outside the circuit, I expressed my dissatisfaction with the situation in the family company and that I was considering breaking away and forming my own company. I told him that I would not countenance forming a competitive caravan equipment business but rather a caravan manufacturing company even though I had no personal experience of building caravans. He kindly offered there and then to loan me £1000.00 to help start the new venture, but on reflection I realised that with my family commitments the only viable alternative was to start a business in which I had considerable experience, namely caravan equipment. I therefore wrote to him in May turning down his generous offer.

In August 1966, I completed a résumé of all sections of the business currently pursued and its future prospects. The company had no capital and although sales on the wholesale side had increased, trading conditions had become extremely difficult and I believed drastic urgent action was required. I recommended that we sell the Manchester premises and move out, preferably westwards towards North Wales, and rent property whilst retaining the capital from the sale of the factory. It had been built before 1869 for engineering purposes and what was required now was a modern warehouse in a better distribution location to service the requirements of the caravan trade. This was given to my father, who did not respond. On the 31st December 1966, I wrote to him again and gave him my resignation. He did respond this time in writing to advise he was very shocked and in view of my decision had altered his will as he considered he had passed on his knowledge of the caravan industry to me only to be let down. This was true except that his knowledge was about the retail caravan industry and not the trade industry which I had developed myself. I was particularly sorry that my decision would affect him unfairly, because he alone of the third generation was to advance the company in his lifetime by introducing the caravan and trailer side in the 1920s. However, I had no alternative because not only did I believe that the company could not survive without drastic measures, but I had to ensure my own family's future – that of my wife Sheila and four children (Yvonne, Denise, Antony and Timothy) whom I wished to educate privately because state education at the time was a non-starter. Soon after, the family company went bankrupt.

There is no doubt that both my brother Peter and myself benefitted from the opportunity to experience the administration discipline prevalent in a long-established family organisation and it was not unusual for management and staff to become complacent, with the eventual collapse witnessed here.

My father and my brother later formed another company, Harry Lea & Son, with premises on the other side of Rochdale Road with a retail shop and light engineering facilities.

CHAPTER 6

A New Venture

Just prior to resigning, I had discussed the situation again with my friend Alex Bullen and he offered capital for shares in the new company I was to establish. Unfortunately, but understandably, he arranged for his solicitor to write to me to confirm our agreement of 20% of the shares; and they added the proviso that any future developments would also give him 20% of same which had not been mentioned originally. This was not acceptable to myself, and it was now a matter of urgency to find working capital.

We sold our semi detached house in Bramhall and purchased a smaller house in Marple Bridge. This released £2000.00. I now called on several friends and acquaintances, both privately and in the trade to obtain the finance for the initial stock. One of these was Tommy Marshall of Peak Trailers of Stockport who had no hesitation in loaning me £500.00 on the shake of a hand over a pint of beer in the local pub. With this generosity, it should be borne in mind the value of this loan today after more than forty years of inflation.

Tommy was a rough diamond who I had met earlier in Hazel Grove, and was a legendary character in the caravan industry. He had built up Peak Trailers in a remarkably short time and there were many stories about him. The one I always remember was the time he was stopped by the police for speeding on a regular journey to Hull, the home of the caravan industry. He had an appointment with the boss of Kingston (AC) Limited who had just been made the Sheriff of Hull. Tommy was confident that he would be able to squash the forthcoming speeding charge, but the new Sheriff said he could not interfere. In exasperation Tommy allegedly stated, 'You may be the Sheriff of Hull, but I am the Marshall of Stockport and I would get you off!' He was to buy a caravan park in Bantry Bay in the Republic of Ireland. On one of his trips there, in his privately owned aircraft, he flew into a Welsh mountain in bad weather and did not survive.

In spite of turning down the offer of capital from my friend Alex Bullen, he now gave me £250.00 on a promissory note. Then my father-in-law loaned me another £250.00 and I was pleased to be able to repay him within a few months. Therefore, I started with £3000.00 of stock. In due course, I was helped by several customers with early settlement of their accounts and particularly by Belmont Caravans of

Hull whose owners Peter Adams and Dave Weinberg paid for goods initially on a pro-forma invoice basis before delivery. Even so, the project would not have survived without the good references I received from several suppliers which enabled me to obtain credit terms. Typical was one from Whyman's Foundry shown here.

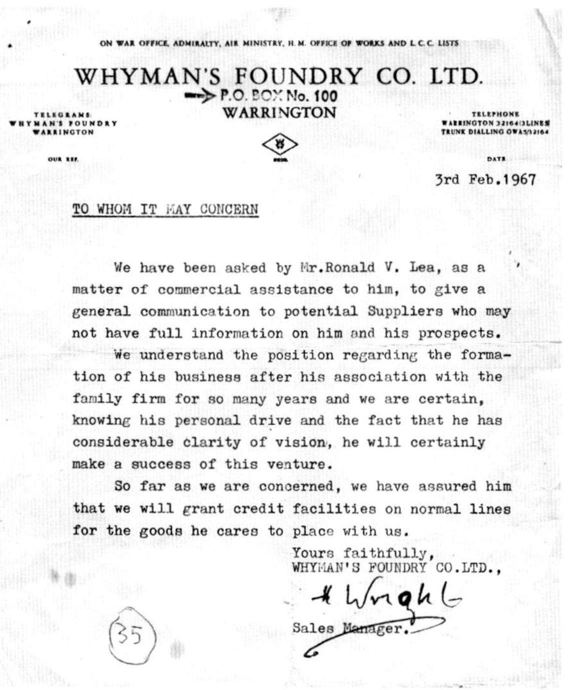

ON WAR OFFICE, ADMIRALTY, AIR MINISTRY, H. M. OFFICE OF WORKS AND L. C. C. LISTS

WHYMAN'S FOUNDRY CO. LTD.
P.O. BOX No. 100
WARRINGTON

TELEGRAMS:
WHYMAN'S FOUNDRY
WARRINGTON

TELEPHONE
WARRINGTON 32164 (3 LINES)
TRUNK DIALLING OWA5/32164

OUR REF.

DATE
3rd Feb.1967

TO WHOM IT MAY CONCERN

We have been asked by Mr.Ronald V. Lea, as a matter of commercial assistance to him, to give a general communication to potential Suppliers who may not have full information on him and his prospects.

We understand the position regarding the formation of his business after his association with the family firm for so many years and we are certain, knowing his personal drive and the fact that he has considerable clarity of vision, he will certainly make a success of this venture.

So far as we are concerned, we have assured him that we will grant credit facilities on normal lines for the goods he cares to place with us.

Yours faithfully,
WHYMAN'S FOUNDRY CO.LTD.,

Sales Manager.

Example of a typical business reference received by the author in 1967

Professional people who knew me personally, and had confidence in my integrity, were approached, including John Burgess, manager of the District Bank in Stockport who knew me through his brother-in-law Alex Bullen who opened an account for the new company. I was to recollect his parting words to me eleven years later when the National Westminster Bank was to put a receiver into a successful caravan manufacturing company I had formed in Hull: 'If you are in difficulties at any time in the future, always insist that the district manager grants you the opportunity to discuss the matter face-to-face, even if you have to sit outside his office door until he agrees.' Unfortunately, when this time came, John was then North-West Director of the National Westminster Bank and Ascot Caravans Limited was in Hull which came under the North-East Director and the personal contact was lost. Ronald V Lea Limited was incorporated on the 16th February 1967.

1969 - Ron and Sheila with staff and employees as they gather outside the Croft at Compstall Mills

I had been looking for a property in Stockport, but there was nothing suitable. Eventually, the agent suggested a property in Compstall, a village a few miles to the east where Compstall Mills Estate had a building vacant known as The Croft, where the looms were kept for the mill. Because it had not been used for many years, it was inundated with birds which had been nesting there for generations and this resulted, in due course, in a problem of soiled stock. Also the noise was overpowering. On one particular occasion a regular customer telephoned and abruptly stopped talking to me, saying, 'Where the hell are you Ron, in a bloody field?' Soon after, we employed a cat, appropriately named Sooty, who would go up on the gantry and clear all the birds out of the building.

This 7.5 ton Leyland van was very nearly damaged in N. Ireland when the mob in Bobbie Sands village attacked it

Eighty-seven and a half percent of the shares in the new company were held by me and 12.5% by my wife Sheila. Even before hardly any stock had been received, I started to call on customers with a second-hand Ford Transit van we had purchased whilst my wife remained in a virtually empty warehouse doing limited office work and taking essential phone calls. It was some months before our first employee arrived. John Burnell had been my office manager at Joseph Lea and decided to join us even though it meant moving his residence. The turnover when I left Joseph Lea & Sons Limited was in the region of £160,000.00 and in the eleven months up to the 31st December 1967 the turnover of the new company was nearly £60,000.00. Most importantly, however, the latter made a net profit of just over £4000.00, whereas the old company made a considerable loss on its larger turnover. In the next twelve months up to 31st December 1968, the new company sales were £160,000.00 with a net profit of £15,569.00, in 1969 £180,000.00, in 1970 £278,000.00 and then more than £391,000.00 in 1971 with a gross profit of more than £70,000.00. Corporation tax at this time was at least 40% which was a crippling amount for a new company trying to build for the future. Over this period, overheads had increased substantially including further staff, amongst whom were the travelling salesman, Norman Crick, and our warehouse manager, Mike Reynolds, formerly employed by Joseph Lea & Sons Limited. Joe Sloan, a local man, had a Class One HGV licence and was employed to drive the tractor with articulated trailers. Later he became our sales representative.

The Seddon 13/4 tractor unit with Perkins engine which I drove to Macclesfield to show my brother WITHOUT the articulated trailer attached

By 1971, the company was employing fourteen people including two sales representatives, van drivers, warehouse packers and a warehouse foreman, plus a warehouse manager. Company transport consisted of a new 13/4 Seddon tractor unit with two articulated box trailers, a four-ton box van and three light vans, two being used by representatives, a 1300 cc Austin for the manager, and I ran an Austin A55 estate car. All the printing was done in-house to reduce costs and facilitate price amendments. An illustrated catalogue had not been produced at this time, although it was expected to be available for the new season. Because of the shortage of space, a platform had been erected to give extra storage space and the owners of the building had agreed to provide a new extension.

Transit box van which company representatives used prior to being replaced by Morris Marina Estate cars

Before this, however, we had changed two of the light vans for Morris Marina estate cars for the company representatives who required the load capacity to take samples of our best sellers to show customers. They covered a high mileage and when we needed to replace them the local main dealer for BMC could only supply saloons because the estate version could not be produced owing to a strike at the factory. This was the period of disruption caused by the union led by 'Red Robbo', and in desperation, I part-exchanged our Marina estates for Fiat Mirafiori estates, and when they arrived (three of them, including one for the new sales manager), I photographed them and sent them with a covering letter for the personal attention of Robinson, the shop steward, advising that we could not buy British as desired through their intransigence and suggesting their attitude would ruin the British motor industry which, of course, eventually it was to do.

One of the Morris Marina Estate cars photographed and sent to 'Red Robbo'

Although we had some export business, the potential was very great and with the extra capacity of the warehouse, we intended to expand into Europe and Scandinavia. Prior to the introduction of import deposits, we were negotiating with several overseas suppliers, including the International Oil Burner Company of Missouri, USA, who were the principle suppliers of mobile home heater/air-conditioning units, and these negotiations were ongoing. The new company had also been offered an agency by Perkins Boilers of Derby which we had not taken up, but was still available if desired.

The prospect of sales in the future was very encouraging. The profit and loss account on the balance sheet showed we had made 18% gross profit in sales, but the bottom line was that we had made less than 4% net profit. Corporation tax at 40% showed there had been no opportunity to build up reserve funds for a rainy day which would almost certainly come in the future.

Through my personal connections with the owners of caravan manufacturing companies, I found that most of them were making substantial profits and Cresta Caravans, now a subsidiary of the Pemberton Group near Wigan, making static holiday caravans, was one of the most successful. When I first called on Pemberton, I used to see Norman Rigby who appeared to be in charge, but later it suddenly became his brother, Eric Rigby, that made the decisions and Norman was not to be seen. I was told later that these two brothers who owned the company between them had a difference of opinion and decided to settle the matter by a fist fight in the yard behind the offices which the ex-'wall-of-death' rider Eric won, and thereafter was always in charge. An unusual but forthright system of management!

The manager of the Cresta factory in Hull was Clifford Sproson and it was a very efficient and profitable extension of the main unit from the figures I obtained. I therefore suggested to Clifford that with his expertise on the production side and my experience with financial and sales side, we would be a combination to run a very successful company. He was very interested in the proposal and in 1971 we started to meet half-way between Hull and Compstall at the Monk Fryston Hotel near Selby, North Yorkshire, to plan this new project.

I realised that my decision to become involved in caravan manufacturing would jeopardise the sales of equipment to static holiday caravan manufacturers which I had developed over the years, but these sales were reduced as they became much larger units with greater buying powers and only selected business became available to Arleigh. I did not expect it to affect the tourer caravan manufacturers or the mobile home manufacturers, with only one exception. Welton Coachcraft were quality touring caravan manufacturers, only a few miles from the proposed Ascot factory at North Cave. Gordon Robson, with his brother David, owned the company and Gordon's family joined my family at a hotel on the side of Lake Ullswater in the Lake District on Easter holidays over several years.

When he heard of my new venture, he warned me that if Ascot 'poached' any of his staff he would stop dealing with Arleigh. This was unlikely because his company were makers of luxury units with a completely different specification whereas Ascot were mass-produced units for a different market and I gave him my assurance and our relationship was not affected. However, prior to this, I had been unable to persuade him to fit a stainless steel sink and drainer unit which I was to sell later to the much larger manufacturer Ace Caravans. Their much higher priced caravans deserved better quality equipment.

However, he did introduce me to a neighbour who was the Captain of the *Norland* ferry owned by North Sea Ferries (now P&O) sailing from Hull to Zeebrugge. When on sales missions for Ascot Caravans (Exports) Ltd, I would travel on the *Norland* when Captain Don Ellerby invited me to the officers' dining room for a meal with him and his staff. On another occasion, he invited me onto the ship's bridge as he manoeuvred this large vessel into this ancient port. His obvious seafaring skills were confirmed by the MoD when he took the

2nd Parachute Battalion and military equipment down to the Falklands War in the early 80s on the *Norland* which in view of its rough sea instability was quite a feat of seamanship. He was awarded the CBE.

Prior to me leaving the family company, my father, brother and myself had formed another company with an ageing Uncle Joe in the builder’s merchant trade, Harpson Wholesale. This was to facilitate the purchase of normal household products on the right terms, as the mobile home manufacturers were increasingly using domestic products as their units become larger. To take advantage of this increasing trade I now formed Arleigh Equipment Ltd at the same premises as the Arleigh caravan equipment company with its own staff including my brother’s eldest son, Nigel Lea, who was to work in different departments.

CHAPTER 7

Expansion into Manufacturing

On the 19th of June 1972, a new company, Ascot Caravan Company Limited, was established in the village of North Cave just west of Hull. Cliff had found a suitable property in which we could produce about twenty caravans per week. However, this depended on renting a small plot of land at the rear of the premises from a local farmer so that through-put for the production line could be established, and this I was able to arrange. In the first eighteen months sales period up to 31st December 1973, turnover was a total of £855,000.00 with a gross profit of more than £135,000.00, net profit of £83,000.00.

Some time later, we formed another company to facilitate exports, Ascot Caravans (Exports) Limited and at the end of June 1977, the total turnover of the two companies was £2,199,483.00 with a net profit of £232,198.00.

The first production Ascot static holiday caravan outside the factory in N.Cave

At this time, I was attending both companies during the week, Ronald V Lea Limited on a Monday and a Friday/Saturday, driving to Ascot on a Tuesday morning and leaving Thursday afternoon. Both companies were flourishing, the former using the trade name Arleigh, a corruption of my name R. Lea, and the new company in Yorkshire was particularly doing well, so much so that it was decided between Cliff and myself that a new larger factory was required and enquiries were made on Sutton Fields industrial estate. The land was owned by the council who were renting out different premises, but we insisted that we would only buy, not rent, and were able to erect a purpose-made caravan factory. We therefore bought eight acres of land at £12,500.00 per acre and built a factory specifically for the mass production (up to 100 units per week) of static holiday caravans and obtained a loan of £90,000.00 from The County Bank, a subsidiary of the National Westminster. We entered the factory in September 1975.

Aerial photograph of the new Ascot factory showing administration offices adjacent

The new companies in Hull continued to expand, particularly the export sales. Our agent on the continent was the Wearing Brothers in Holland and Zeebrugge Caravans in Belgium. The latter company was distributing other British caravan makes, and therefore our own sales were restricted through them. On a visit to Belgium I was approached by one of the salesmen at Zeebrugge Caravans whose name was Jacques Hendrix, with a view to him becoming a salesman with our company. I did not respond at the time in deference to the association with his employer, Zeebrugge Caravans, and whilst awaiting the ferry to return to England, he arrived at the port in much haste before I left. I made arrangements with him to visit the factory in Hull to discuss the matter further. On making enquiries, we found that he had a good reputation as a salesman and his enthusiasm was clearly genuine. However, what we were to learn later was that, according to Belgian friends, he was 'hungry when his belly is full', suggesting that his aspirations could tempt him into a nefarious situation.

Opening day of new Ascot factory on Sutton Fields Industrial Estate – September 1975

We bought land at Nivelles in Belgium to store our stock and set up two of our largest mobile units as offices. We then formed a new company, Ascot International SA. This Belgian company was supplied by Ascot Caravans (Exports) Limited. At this time, corporation tax was 52% of profits. We had approximately 120 employees at the Hull factory, the whole of the new purpose-built factory was designed for maximum production capacity, three of our largest mobile units were sited and adjacent outside and used as offices: a general sales/accounts office, an office for Cliff Sproson, and an office for myself which was fitted out with living facilities.

Meanwhile, sales were developing quickly in Belgium; we had bought Jacques Hendrix a Mercedes Benz saloon car and he was travelling further afield, particularly in France. Later, when sales developed even further, we replaced the Mercedes Benz with a new Jaguar XJ6 saloon. By this time we had approximately ten employees at the Nivelles depot, including an accountant, Emile Gendarme, office manager and another salesman.

Cliff Sproson and myself decided that we would personally investigate the prospects in France, which was clearly the largest market on the continent. We joined Jacques Hendrix in his Jaguar and travelled down to the South of France. One of our French customers had arranged a meal at Paul Bocuse's famous restaurant at Lyons, where we were introduced to the famous restaurateur. We carried on to Fréjus and saw other customers before arranging with one of the caravan parks to accept the siting of two of our largest units for use by our families in the future.

Sheila Lea, Addie Sproson, Clifford Sproson and Ron Lea celebrate a successful 1977 season at the Paris Caravan Exhibition

Because of the likely expansion into the South of France and even into Spain, I decided to learn to fly and started having lessons at Paull Airfield near Hull with a female instructor. I particularly remember her frustration when landing the single-engine monoplane to have another plane cut across in front, which was greeted with an expletive, 'B— Battle of Britain twits'. Many of the pilots were veterans of that great victory that saved our country. I never completed the course after serious circumstances affected the existence of the company.

At this time, our caravans were exported from Harwich to Zeebrugge in British Rail ships and to check out how they were being handled, I took the opportunity with my wife to travel on one of the voyages. Whilst they looked after our caravans very well, the personal accommodation was hardly luxurious! Initially, the caravans were stored at Zeebrugge on the port docks until transport from our Nivelles depot could collect them. On one occasion whilst in storage, a storm force wind developed and a substantial number of caravans were damaged because they had been parked too close together. They were still able to be collected by our Nivelles transport, but then had to be repaired before they could be sold. This accident of nature was the beginning of our knowledge of a conspiracy of fraud.

The Onedin Line

. . . for the executive

CHARLOTTE RHODES – The original Onedin Line topsail schooner

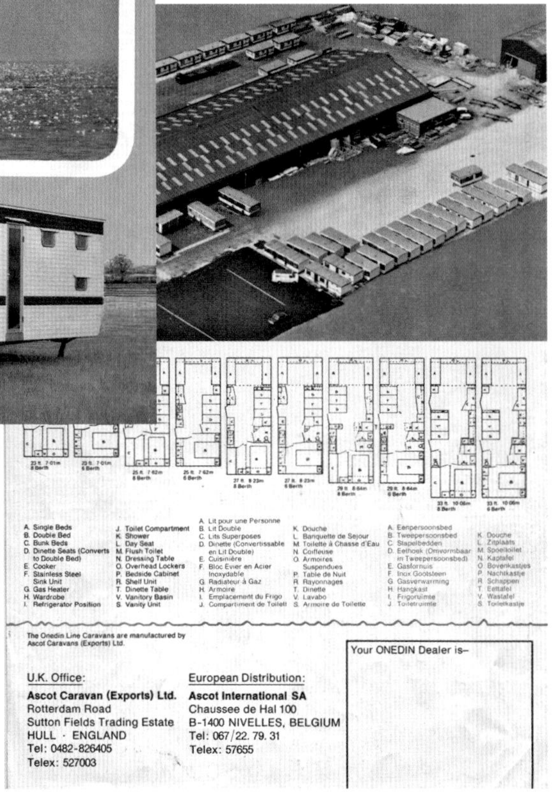

23 ft. 7·01m 8 Berth | 23 ft. 7·01m 6 Berth | 25 ft. 7·62m 8 Berth | 25 ft. 7·62m 6 Berth | 27 ft. 8·23m 8 Berth | 27 ft. 8·23m 6 Berth | 29 ft. 8·84m 8 Berth | 29 ft. 8·84m 6 Berth | 33 ft. 10·06m 8 Berth | 33 ft. 10·06m 6 Berth

A. Single Beds
B. Double Bed
C. Bunk Beds
D. Dinette Seats (Converts to Double Bed)
E. Cooker
F. Stainless Steel Sink Unit
G. Gas Heater
H. Wardrobe
I. Refrigerator Position
J. Toilet Compartment
K. Shower
L. Day Seat
M. Flush Toilet
N. Dressing Table
O. Overhead Lockers
P. Bedside Cabinet
R. Shelf Unit
T. Dinette Table
V. Vanitory Basin
S. Vanity Unit

A. Lit pour une Personne
B. Lit Double
C. Lits Superposes
D. Dinette (Convertissable en Lit Double)
E. Cuisinière
F. Bloc Evier en Acier Inoxydable
G. Radiateur à Gaz
H. Armoire
I. Emplacement du Frigo
J. Compartiment de Toilett
K. Douche
L. Banquette de Sejour
M. Toilette à Chasse d'Eau
N. Coiffeuse
O. Armoires Suspendues
P. Table de Nuit
R. Rayonnages
T. Dinette
V. Lavabo
S. Armoire de Toilette

A. Eenpersoonsbed
B. Tweepersoonsbed
C. Stapelbedden
D. Eethoek (Omvormbaar in Tweepersoonsbed)
E. Gasfornuis
F. Inox Gootsteen
G. Gasverwarming
H. Hangkast
I. Frigoruimte
J. Toiletruimte
K. Douche
L. Zitplaats
M. Spoeltoilet
N. Kaptafel
O. Bovenkastjes
P. Nachtkastje
R. Schappen
T. Eettafel
V. Wastafel
S. Toiletkastje

The Onedin Line Caravans are manufactured by Ascot Caravans (Exports) Ltd.

Your ONEDIN Dealer is–

U.K. Office:
Ascot Caravan (Exports) Ltd.
Rotterdam Road
Sutton Fields Trading Estate
HULL · ENGLAND
Tel: 0482-826405
Telex: 527003

European Distribution:
Ascot International SA
Chaussee de Hal 100
B-1400 NIVELLES, BELGIUM
Tel: 067/22. 79. 31
Telex: 57655

Some of the models produced in the Ascot factory

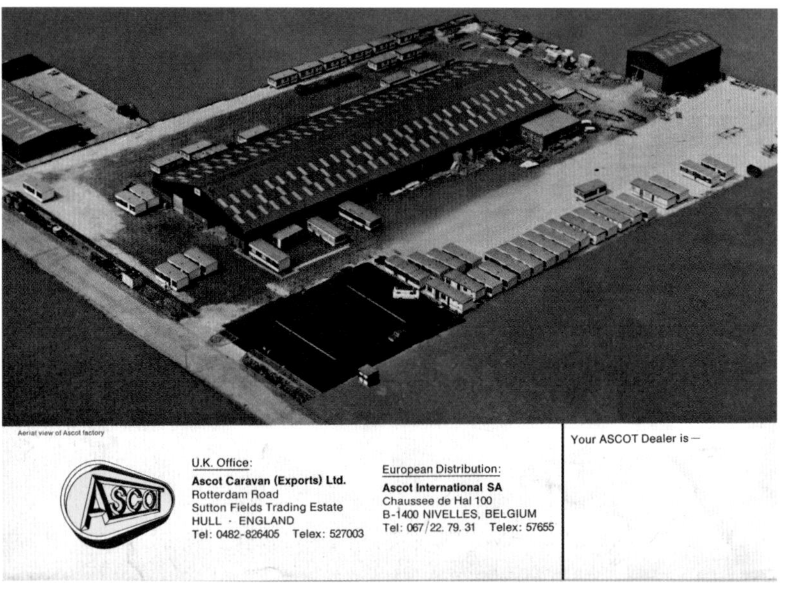

Aerial view of Ascot factory

U.K. Office:
Ascot Caravan (Exports) Ltd.
Rotterdam Road
Sutton Fields Trading Estate
HULL · ENGLAND
Tel: 0482-826405 Telex: 527003

European Distribution:
Ascot International SA
Chaussee de Hal 100
B-1400 NIVELLES, BELGIUM
Tel: 067/22. 79. 31 Telex: 57655

Your ASCOT Dealer is –

CHAPTER 8

Conspiracy of Fraud in Belgium

It was necessary for skilled practical workmen from the factory to visit Nivelles and repair the caravans. Two brothers, both workshop foremen, were delegated for this work and soon after they arrived were entertained by the directeur général, Jacques Hendrix, and the accountant Emile Gendarme at a local nightclub. During the evening these two fraudsters suggested that anything they saw at Nivelles storage depot should not be mentioned to Cliff Sproson or myself, otherwise there would be dire consequences. The two brothers went along with this subterfuge in the short term, repaired the caravans and on their return immediately advised us of the likely criminality at our 100% owned depot in Belgium.

Soon after their return to the UK, my good friend and company accountant, Reuben Kay and myself caught a BEA flight to Brussels and endeavoured to trace Hendrix and Gendarme, but without success. The Belgium procurator had been informed of these developments and tried to prevent us leaving the country, so that he could discuss the situation. This was of great concern for Reuben Kay, who had a very active accountancy practice to look after so when the return scheduled flight was delayed he hired a private plane at London airport to return to Manchester that evening.

Reuben Kay then arranged for two of his staff to visit Nivelles to take stock of all our caravans. It soon became apparent on checking our despatch chassis numbers at the factory with the stock that there was a considerable discrepancy. Soon after one of the three conspirators, a caravan dealer in the area contacted Cliff Sproson and myself at the factory to arrange a secret meeting in one of the hotels in Brussels. He had obviously got 'cold feet' and as he could not speak English it was necessary to arrange for an interpreter by contacting Madame Schwind at our solicitors, Paul Lauwyers, who arranged for her son to act in this way. The meeting took place in a quiet bedroom when he admitted to receiving stolen caravans from our depot in collaboration with Mr Hendrix and Mr Gendarme, obviously hoping that his confession would alleviate guilt and the punishment that was certainly forthcoming. The authorities were informed and the trial took place and all three of the conspirators were sentenced to jail.

Although we had successfully stopped the thefts of our caravans it was too late to save the company. For some months previously, I had become aware of a deterioration in cash flow from Ascot International SA, which was difficult to be certain because they were factoring their invoices. We were also under pressure from the National Westminster Bank who had arranged a loan with their subsidiary County Bank to buy a new factory. During this period, I had meetings with the National Westminster area manager in Hull and on one occasion he asked me if I knew what a long firm fraud meant; I replied that I had no idea. On return to Arleigh, I telephoned (as usual in this crisis period) our accountant Reuben Kay and told him of the unusual statement of the area manager, to which he replied he meant 'a long term fraud'.

They unrealistically believed that we were fraudulently retaining payment for these caravans sold in Belgium and were to arrange an investigation through their Brussels associate bank. In due course, they appointed a receiver at the head office of Ascot Caravans Ltd and Ascot Caravan Exports Ltd in Hull on the 24th February, 1978. This premature action caused a furore amongst our business associates, including our accountant Reuben Kay, who deemed it so unnecessary and many of his clients closed their accounts with the National Westminster Bank.

This was my first experience of a British bank's lack of vision and understanding of the special financial requirements of static holiday manufacturers different to other sections of the industry, i.e. mobile home manufacturers. They know very little about commerce and the crisis in the financial world in the twenty-first century is now well known. To give an example it was regular practice for a manufacturer of static holiday caravans to keep employment going over the winter when there was no deliveries to build up stock to meet the demand which commenced in the spring. By the end of February 1978, the orders in house were substantial for delivery in March and April. It was during this period that I telephoned John Prescott, the Labour MP for East Hull, to ask if anything could be done in view of the bank's precipitous action in appointing a receiver and advising him we had 120 employees about to lose their jobs, most of them young men with families. His response was very disappointing, suggesting we the directors and owners would not be out of work for long and making no recommendation whatsoever on how the workforce could be helped. His attitude was like a shop steward, militant and without compassion for these men.

At the creditors' meeting held in Manchester, I was interviewed by David Davies, a BBC commentator at the time and later the chief executive of the Football Association, which was filmed and later broadcast on BBC TV News, in which I explained how this unnecessary situation had evolved.

When the Receipts and Payments account was received from the liquidator the final figures showed that more than £682,000.00 was received and payments made of more than £655,000.00 including £55,000.00 legal charges, £102,000.00 corporation tax, £324,000.00 to unsecured creditors (one creditor told me he had been paid twice!); £120,000.00 remuneration account – remuneration to whom? Leaving a surplus balance of £27,000.00. Without these horrendous expenses the figures proved that forcing the company into administration was completely unnecessary and that it was not only the conspirators who were enriched, but also the bank and the legal people. Soon after these figures became known, the North East Director of the National Westminster Bank invited our accountant Reuben Kay to lunch, at which he confessed that they had acted precipitously.

Although I could personally return to Arleigh at Compstall Mills my co-managing director at Ascot asked me if I would join him again and form another static holiday caravan manufacturing company, I declined because I was devastated by the unprincipled action of the bank and could not foresee ever again relying on money borrowed from any bank and, in fact, never again was I to have a loan from such an unreliable source. Cliff Sproson was to go ahead and form Aquila Caravans which soon after was forced into administration leaving Arleigh amongst its creditors. Cliff was to die in 2005 aged eighty-four years.

CHAPTER 9

Return to Compstall Mills

Returning to my original company in full-time employment, I soon found that whilst trade sales under the name Arleigh were continuing satisfactorily, the cash flow had become more difficult. Soon after, we had a break-in burglary in the warehouse when many items were stolen. There was a suspicion that one or more employees were involved and I decided to make enquiries myself before bringing the police in. I was referred to a private detective by friends and asked Derry Kennearley, an Irishman who had been in the Royal Canadian Mounted Police and now returned to England, to make investigations on my behalf.

By becoming involved in these suspected persons' private lives, e.g. visiting the public houses where one of the drivers involved, lubricated by an excess of liquor, was to boast about his involvement in the conspiracy of theft at Ronald V Lea Limited. Derry made other enquiries so that we had enough evidence to refer the matter to the Regional Crime Squad. It turned out that the warehouse foreman, a warehouse packer and this particular van driver had been stealing caravan equipment over a period of time and selling it wherever they could. In fact, it turned out that the warehouse foreman had purchased a tourer caravan on these unearned proceeds and fitted it out with all possible stolen caravan equipment, and when its location was established, Derry and myself went down to the south coast to pick it up and tow it back to Compstall Mills. In due course, these three conspirators were found guilty at a Manchester court and sentenced to jail. The police had recovered a van load of this stolen caravan equipment, but the exact amount and value over an unknown period of time was never established, but it was another case of the perpetrators being apprehended, but leaving the company in a dire financial position.

Therefore, in 1981, I decided that The Croft should become a cash and carry warehouse and so obtain retail cash sales to alleviate the problem. However, this was too late to save the company. Therefore, Etherow Leisure Centre was founded on the 5th May 1981 to facilitate these sales, but unfortunately, the original company, Ronald V Lea Limited, went into administration on the 28th of July 1982. Probably because we were off the 'beaten track' the cash sales were disappointing although the trade sales established over more than fifteen years

A later photograph when known as ARLEIGH showing the extension to the building and the gantry to the original building which facilitated the unloading of cast iron and asbestos pipes and the loading of completed combined flue assemblies. Jaguar Series III E-Type roadster restored by Garage Manager Don Law for Peter Sutherland of the Sutherland Food Group family

now under the name Arleigh were encouraging.

During this period, the trade sales were assisted by the sales manager, who was prepared to travel in the evenings so that she was at the customer's door when they opened in the morning. Her name was Carol Drinnan, and this dedication rejuvenated sales to the retail shop outlets, 'first come, first served'. However, an attachment to a Scottish customer resulted in her leaving our employ later when she removed to his area, proving in this instance that male and female are not born equal in business terms. If the sales manager had been male, he would not have been under pressure to leave a good job as under this liaison, his consort would have joined him in Cheshire. So we lost a valuable employee.

I was now free from other business commitments and started to call again on important manufacturer customers and in addition decided to develop the Northern Ireland trade which involved travelling from Compstall Mills to the ferry terminal at Cairnryan in Scotland to Larne in Co. Antrim in my own car every three weeks.

This was at the height of the 'Troubles', but I was only stopped once during the whole period by the 'Green Linnetts', the Ulster Defence Regiment army patrol, although when visiting Paddy Mahon in the Catholic Bogside of Londonderry, I would leave my car and walk to his premises past the Royal Ulster Constabulary's heavily fortified police station with the feeling that I was watched all the way. On arrival I was treated like royalty with the best tea service ready whilst a good order was always forthcoming. The only time I crossed the border was at Letterkenny in the Irish Republic when I called at Johnsons Caravans, a very good customer. Following my visit, a 7.5-ton delivery van would follow my route and on one occasion, after Bobbie Sands had died of starvation in prison, his birthplace was the scene of riots and the driver's route passed through his village which had been cordoned off by the police. For some unknown reason, the driver drove past the cordon and his vehicle was attacked by the mob. The police were quick to react and got him turned round before too much damage had been done. On his return to Compstall Mills, I inspected the vehicle and found a replica revolver in the cab, which was confiscated. Even though it was very realistic it would hardly dissuade the rioting mob and he was not asked to do the Irish trip again.

The garage at The Croft was used for maintenance of all the company vehicles and race preparation of my race cars, and a full time mechanic was employed, Ron Needham. I offered a maintenance service to Jaguar owners and attended an LPG conversion course with Ron Needham. The idea was that we would become stockists of LPG equipment and install same on customers' cars. The initial stock value was quite high, and whilst I deliberated on whether to go ahead with the investment, the UK agent went into liquidation. These plans, therefore, were shelved for the time being. Later Don Law, who had prepared my Jaguar E-Type on a part-time basis, joined the company as a full-time garage manager.

After the demise of Ronald V Lea Limited, there was another break-in by council workers who were employed to lay a new pipeline in front of the property. It was only by chance, on attending the office at the weekend, that I found a white van backed up to the showroom next to the front door that I noticed the window into the showroom had been broken and the thieves were still inside the warehouse. I immediately dialled 999, grabbed a solid fuel stove poker and chased them out of the building. The police arrived quickly enough to arrest the two thieves, but within two or three days one of these was seen by me during office hours, having returned to excavate the ground for the pipe, and I immediately telephoned the council and told them if he was not removed forthwith, I would not be responsible for my actions!

However, before this and when Ron Needham left our employ, I had advertised for a replacement which was answered by Roger Lewis, who arrived for an interview with his father in an Aristocat replica of the Jaguar XK120/140 which he had built himself. I had an opportunity to drive this replica myself, which was originally a Jaguar XJ6 saloon, but the vital dimensions had not been corrected to those of an original early XK sports car, so that the handling was found to be no different to the saloon basis. Roger was very keen on the motor racing aspect of the job and started as garage manager soon after. He was to emigrate to British Columbia and has always kept in touch with me since.

In January 1981, our youngest son, Timothy, joined the company and was soon conversant with running a private commercial business. On the 21st of May, 1986, I decided to change the name of Etherow Leisure Centre Limited to Arleigh (Northern) Limited. In the same year, our eldest son, Tony, joined the company.

The company continued to thrive, but as the lease was due for renewal in 1990 I decided for our long term interest we should buy a property which should be ideal for distribution throughout the country.

The turnover for this year had been £828,552.00 with a gross profit of £267,005.00 and a net profit of £95,482.00. For some time we had been increasing sales to the narrowboat industry commencing with the Torgem solid fuel stove for which we had sole selling rights from the manufacturers Jones & Campbell Limited in Scotland, and this was a factor that I considered when deciding on the area that the new property should be established. Travelling down to the Midlands on more than one occasion, JDC member Clive Brandon was most helpful in searching for property.

It was on the A426 from Rugby to Southam I came across a small industrial estate on the side of the Grand Union Canal near the village of Stockton called the Blue Lias Estate. There was a property which was ideal on this estate and as the owners were on the site, I was able to negotiate with them immediately. Therefore the company moved to these new premises in 1990 and was renamed as Arleigh International Limited. Timothy was appointed managing director and Tony works director, whilst I became chairman.

I decided to semi-retire at this point and retained the garage at the Compstall Mills property in support of my motor racing aspirations. Soon after, I bought an American RV (recreation vehicle) which initially was sited at Redlands Caravan Park a few miles away, when my wife joined me as secretary and wages clerk, later parked outside the new premises at Blue Lias Estate where I was to visit every week for a day or two. The company was to thrive at the new location as it was centrally situated to facilitate distribution. Tim was to revitalise the company by selling off most of the transport and making contract arrangements with next day delivery companies. He also introduced a computerised administration and sales system and a new computerised illustrated catalogue.

As I released control of the running of the company, and with the increasing amount of the government and European legislation affecting commerce, I decided that in future, control of the company should be shared by two of our offspring, Timothy and Denise. Denise was living in France and had become our sales manager on the continent and had been very successful. However, when I put it to her that she should become the sales

Arleigh's new premises at Blue Lias Estate, Stockton, Warwickshire

Fleetwind Flair outside warehouse and connected to all mains services - American RV

Arleigh International Ltd property when the company was sold to Caverdale Group, 1997

Back row left to right: Timothy, Ronald, Antony
Front row left to right: Yvonne, Denise, Sheila

director, which would require residence in the UK, she declined because she wished to remain in France. This would have been an ideal arrangement, because Timothy was an excellent administrator and Denise seemed to have inherited my 'genes' for sales including my 'avant-garde' philosophy when she tempted French customers with large bars of Cadbury's milk chocolate in spite of the alleged aversion on the continent because it does not have the correct amount of cocoa in the ingredients. The French loved it which helped to create the 'entente cordiale' to encourage a good order. It was stored in a freezer box in the company's Renault Clio in which she covered 60,000 km in a sales season. A dedicated work ethic.

Denise gained a BA Honours at Leeds University for French and Business Studies and is a Professeur de la Fédération Française de Hatha Yoga. Timothy was to qualify as a helicopter pilot at the age of 40 years and is now a commercial helicopter captain. Tony was to return to his first love, livestock farming, in the Orkney with Friesian cattle and latterly with Suffolk sheep in Lincolnshire. Yvonne, the only offspring not to work for Arleigh, had the gift of natural vocal ability which in due course saw her receive the Curtis Gold Medal at the Royal Northern College of Music, the Peter Stuyvesant Award at the National Opera Studio and the Miriam Licette Scholarship for twelve months' study at Paris Opera with Janine Reiss. She made her debut at the Glyndebourne Festival and immediately was awarded the Glyndebourne Touring Opera Singer's Award. She was a leading mezzo soprano at her peak and is now a contralto who appears regularly on the concert platform both at home and abroad. She teaches singing at both a private high school and a public school. No doubt because of this connection the author was invited to serve on the Manchester Glyndebourne committee although busy company developments precluded regular attendance.

Having decided to sell Arleigh International Ltd as a going concern with all its property and assets, I advertised it nationally. There were several prospective buyers, but in the end it was sold to the Caverdale Group who paid a substantial sum. At the completion of the sale, the audited figures for the first quarter of 1997 showed a gross profit of £184,098.00 representing 29.3% of turnover and £65,218.00 net profit after tax representing 10.4% of sales. In July 1996 I had a debilitating stroke, but fortunately I was able to complete the sale of the company but my business connection ended after 45 years, but this experience continued to be used in Jaguar-related events.

CHAPTER 10

An Avid Motor Racing Follower

At the 1949 British Grand Prix at Silverstone, I watched the first appearance in a supporting race of the XK120 Jaguars driven by Leslie Johnson (whom I was to meet in France later), Prince Bira and Peter Walker, who was to win at Le Mans with Peter Whitehead two years later.

It was in 1951 that my pal, Peter Howarth, and I started discussing the possibility of visiting the Vingt-Quatre Heures du Mans, the famous twenty-four-hour race in France. We did not have the use of a car at the time, but Peter had a 197 cc Francis-Barnet motorcycle and we debated whether it was up to carrying two persons both well over ten stones, haversack holding a tent and two pannier bags each side of the rear wheel for personal effects. When we heard that Jaguar were entering a team of cars, we decided to risk it, even though we were conscious of the bad state of the French roads only six years after the end of the war.

We caught the Bristol Freighter Air Ferry from Lympne in Kent and landed at Le Touquet in France. We were the only motorcycle on board and there were several cars, including a Ford Zodiac driven by Leslie Johnson, the Jaguar Works driver and also the owner of the ERA factory. Seeing how heavily loaded we were, he kindly offered to give me a lift in his car together with all the baggage. It would have made a considerable difference to the performance of the small capacity motorcycle, but I decided we should continue as we started out, but agreed to his offer to take the baggage in his car. He advised he would leave it in the Healey pit at Le Mans. So we set off from the airfield at a good pace sustained by '*vin ordinaire*' at one shilling a litre (5p). There were no drink-driving laws in those days.

When we arrived at Le Mans, we went to the square in the centre of the town where the organising club had their office, Automobile Club de l'Ouest. With only limited French, we were told to go to the interpreter. Her name was Madame Armstrong and we were to learn later that she had an Anglo-Scottish married name from her husband, an American major who had returned to the USA after the war. We asked her the cost of camping inside the circuit, but we thought it was too expensive. When she saw us hesitating, she suggested we go to her summer residence at La Trugalle, a village some twenty kilometres from Le Mans, and camp in the garden. She gave us directions, but first we had to go to the Healey pit to collect our luggage.

It was here that we met Donald Healey, Stirling Moss, John Eason Gibson, who was to become the BRDC secretary later, and other motor racing luminaries. This was the pit for the Nash Healey which was driven in the race by Tony Rolt and Duncan Hamilton who were to win it in 1953 in the Jaguar C-Type.

Summer residence at La Trugalle

When we arrived at La Trugalle we met Madame Armstrong's daughter, Lesley, with her young son who insisted we could stay in the house and not bother to erect the tent. That evening, Madame Armstrong arrived with armbands for an official photographer and a press pass. On top of all this, we were overwhelmed when she said we could use her Citroën 2CV (*deux chevaux*) to commute to the circuit. This was an ideal car for the rough roads at the time. The official armbands enabled us to roam anywhere in the circuit and the pits and we were in fact down with the drivers with their cars up to five minutes before the start at 4.00 pm in those days, when a line of gendarmes with linked arms cleared everybody from the grid except the drivers. This official status was a priceless opportunity for a couple of motor racing enthusiasts. In retrospect, neither Peter nor I were interested in photography and in any case, we were so heavily laden that no camera was taken and there are no photographic records of this particular trip. The two Peters (Whitehead and Walker) won the race in their Jaguar C-Type. This first win for Jaguar was not to be the last.

The generous Armstrong family - Le Mans 1952, Peter, Andrea, Lesley and son, Madame Armstrong

We not only enjoyed the weekend of racing, particularly as Jaguar had won, but also the wonderful atmosphere generated mainly by the French crowd with the exciting facilities trackside with a boxing booth, strip shows, cabaret and sideshows. One of the more unusual spectacles was a ridge tent sited on the inside of the circuit at the Tertre Rouge bends which was a mobile brothel with a queue of men awaiting their turn! C'est la vie en France 1951.

We were determined to go again in 1952, particularly with Madame Armstrong's generous hospitality, although we were not expecting to take advantage of this other French hospitality! This time we made sure we took a camera although neither Peter nor I were very adept at using it as you can tell from the photographs. My father loaned us his Morris van (model E) this time, which had plenty of luggage space. He had fitted perspex windows in

Ron poses in front of the Mercedes-Benz pit with the Morris van - model E

the side walls with Claytonrite rubber so that it was similar to an estate car. This time we went on the ferry from Folkestone to Dieppe.

On arrival at Le Mans, we went straight to the Automobile Club de l'Ouest to meet up with Madame Armstrong and she provided similar official armbands as before. The previous year she had refused any offer of payment for the accommodation at La Trugalle, so this time we brought groceries from England which were not available in France so soon after the war. Over the race weekend we were to see more of her daughter, Lesley, and her little boy, but also a close friend from Dieppe, a teacher of English called Andrea Dumas.

The race debacle of the Jaguar team has been recorded in detail, with all the cars out of action with overheating within a few hours.

En route to Le Mans, when I was driving, I glanced in the interior mirror and saw a line of Jaguar C-Types with a Mark VII saloon supporting car behind catching up very fast. As they came closer the road suddenly switched from the usual straight Rue Nationale to a series of S-bends and they suddenly closed up, but they could not pass. As the road became straight again, they changed down a gear and shot past with the Mark VII in hot pursuit, an exciting recollection even after all these years.

I lost much interest in the race when all the Jaguar Team cars retired, but I particularly remember Alberto Ascari taking the Dunlop Curve after the pits in one long drift with just a flicker of brake lights on his 2.7-litre Ferrari Coupe. After the disaster befalling the Jaguars the French crowd had an even greater disappointment when Pierre Levegh driving his 4.5-litre Lago Talbot single-handed for twenty-three hours was to blow up the engine by selecting the wrong gear through exhaustion, and thus allowing the Mercedes Benz 300 SL gullwing coupes to come first and second. Not a popular result after France had been occupied by the Germans only seven years earlier. Undoubtedly influenced by this, the Mercedes factory offered Pierre Levegh a seat in one of the 300 SLR Team Cars in 1955, with tragic results when he hit a car (Austin Healey) he was lapping driven by Lance Macklin (the son of Sir Noel Macklin, founder of Invicta Cars) and crashed into the public enclosure bank killing himself and eighty-three spectators.

Peter serves an English afternoon tea to Andrea and Lesley - Le Mans 1952

Early overheating problems in the streamline Jaguar C-type

Another overheating Jaguar in the pits

Pierre Levegh passes the pits in his 4½ litre Lago-Talbot soon after to crash with exhaustion after driving 23 hours solo

Alberto Ascari in the Ferrari coupe at full speed approaching the Dunlop bridge - Le Mans 1952

Wishful thinking by the author - Ascari's very quick 2.7 litre Ferrari

Alberto Ascari warms up the 2 litre Ferrari at Spa Francorchamps-World Champion in 1952

Team mate Guiseppe Farina receives instructions, Spa, 1952

The field approach Eau Rouge corner at the start. European Grand Prix, 1952

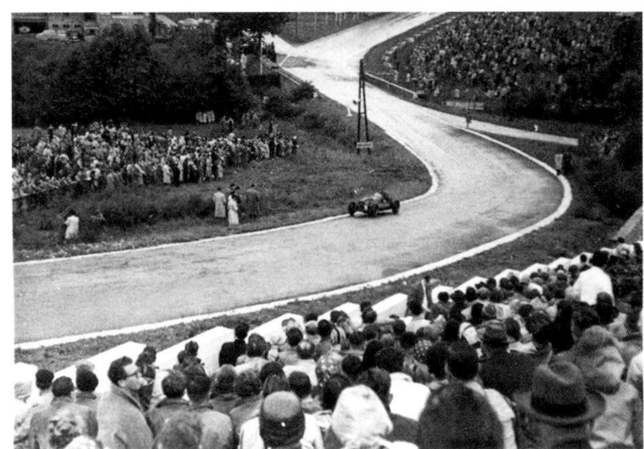

A lonely Mike Hawthorn (Cooper-Bristol) at Eau Rouge, 4th overall in his first continental Grand Prix, 1952

Novel transport for Ron in Spa Francorchamps Park. European Grand Prix, 1952

This time, with the reasonable comfort of a car compared to a motorcycle, we decided to go on to the European Grand Prix held at Spa Francorchamps in Belgium, stopping off in 'Gay' Paris on the way. At Spa this was the first time I saw the new British star racing driver Mike Hawthorn, a sensation at Goodwood earlier in the year. He was to come fourth in his race, his first visit to the Continent, behind the three works Ferraris, Alberto Ascari, Giuseppe Farina and Luigi Villoresi. Ascari was now World Champion. When he was at Silverstone in 1948, he was second to Villoresi, learning his trade from him.

It was at Spa that I started to obtain autographs of the leading drivers in my pigskin cigarette case. I was a regular cigarette smoker at the time when I had the idea of taking all the cigarettes out and asking them to sign the inside with a ballpoint pen. Ascari, Farina, Villoresi and Hawthorn all agreed to this novel idea and were the first autographs obtained during practice. These were complemented later by Juan-Manuel Fangio, Stirling Moss, Mark Webber, Martin Brundle and Sir Jackie Stewart. This is a valuable piece of memorabilia.

On the return journey through France, we came across an American military convoy of about six vehicles driving nose-to-tail. The leading vehicle had a spot lamp on top of the cab pointing rearwards with a soldier standing by it flashing the lamp every time the lead vehicle braked. In this way, the rearmost vehicle was able to brake virtually at the same time as did all the others and keep up a speed of some fifty to sixty mph nose-to-tail, which made it very difficult to pass the convoy. Eventually I made it by doing the maximum speed that the Morris van was capable of (seventy mph). Why did they use such a method? I believe this was because the French had such a reputation for 'do or die' driving that if they had left a space between their vehicles, a French vehicle could split up the convoy and cause disruption. To confirm this theory, I had seen a cartoon at the time depicting an American officer with his helmeted men gathered round with trucks in the background. The caption stated 'Some of you men will not come back, there is a French convoy on the road.' I was reminded of this event in 2004 when the RAC crew of the breakdown lorry called out to attend a burst trailer tyre on the M25 motorway (I was returning from the 'War and Peace' show where John Pearson and myself had been promoting the England/Hawthorn Memorial with the new Jaguar X-Type saloon selling raffle tickets), when they warned me to beware of French lorry drivers in particular.

Following the 1952 Le Mans and European Grand Prix at Spa Francorchamps, Peter and I were so impressed by Mike Hawthorn's fourth place in his first Grand Prix that we decided to see how he went on in his next race in a mixed-formula event at Boreham, near Chelmsford in Essex.

He had entered the same 2-litre Cooper Bristol and was up against the two V16 BRMs driven by José Froilán González and Ken Wharton and two 4.5-litre Ferraris driven by Luigi Villoresi and Chico Landi. We were both supporters of BRM, but were becoming disillusioned when they kept breaking down. Because it was going to take some time to get to Boreham in the model E Morris van we left Cheshire the night before in the pouring rain and parked outside the circuit gates. After a disturbed night sleeping in the van it was still raining when the main race started.

A very wet Guy Entwistle surveys the scene - Le Mans 1954

Although on the front row of the grid, González went off at the first corner through the straw bales and was not seen again. He was a greatly underrated driver, but the V16 engine power curve was virtually impossible to control in these conditions. Meanwhile, Mike Hawthorn had taken the lead and was pulling away from the two Ferraris. Unfortunately for him, it stopped raining and the Ferrari drivers were able to use their considerable power advantage to overtake so that in the end he finished third.

He was also third in the British Grand Prix at Silverstone later behind the Ferraris of Ascari and Villoresi. The following year I went to the British Empire Trophy held in Douglas, Isle of Man, although the Jaguar C-Types entered were not successful. It is mainly remembered for a 'prima donna' display to a sceptical youth (yours truly) by Raymond Mays on the ship from Liverpool to Douglas. I did not introduce myself as he obviously expected. He was accompanying Reg Parnell who was going to demonstrate the V16 BRM during the race interval.

I had missed the 1953 Le Mans Race which Duncan Hamilton and Tony Rolt would win so convincingly in the Jaguar C-Type, but I went again in 1954 with another friend, the late Guy Entwistle in his Ford-engine kit car.

An original painting by Terence Cuneo of F.R.W. 'Lofty' England supervising a pit stop at Le Mans in 1953 and dedicated 'To Ron, then and always a great Jaguar man, Lofty 6/6/1991'

When we arrived at the Automobile Club de l'Ouest we found that Madame Armstrong had left the club's employment and therefore we could not get the valuable official armbands enjoyed previously. Fortunately we had brought a tent for camping and erected it inside the circuit. It rained torrentially over the weekend and without an official pass we had no cover whilst viewing and spent most of the time over the Jaguar pits. In fact, to retain our front line position here, we stayed most of the night and were absolutely soaked.

The only relieving excitement was the gallant attempts by Tony and Duncan in the Jaguar D-Type to catch the 4.9-litre Ferrari V12 being driven by Maurice Trintignant. Towards the end, Tony Rolt was catching him 'hand over fist' and unlapped himself. He made signals to 'Lofty' England the Jaguar pit manager that he required a visor in the atrocious conditions instead of the goggles he was wearing. Lofty decided

The gallant Jaguar D-Type in second place by 2 minutes after 24 hours - Le Mans 1954

that he would get his co-pilot prepared to take over complete with visor and Tony was brought in for the changeover. Although I had great admiration for Duncan Hamilton's courage, I believed Tony Rolt was a quicker driver in these conditions and I was surprised at this development. Much later when I got to know Lofty England, I asked him why he had made this decision to change the drivers and not just hand Tony a visor without him getting out of the car. He advised that he thought, on balance, it would be preferable to substitute a fully rested Duncan as Tony Rolt had been driving for some time in these very bad conditions. Meanwhile, the Ferrari had been brought into the pits for Froilán González to take over, but the car would not restart. After what seemed like an interminable period with a car surrounded by an illegal number of frantic mechanics, the engine fired at last and he was away. González was one of the leading Grand Prix drivers at the time and Duncan Hamilton with the Jaguar could not catch him and finished some two minutes behind after twenty-four hours.

Although my motorsport activities were inevitably limited following my marriage in 1955 and a family of four children by the early 1960s, I still followed motor racing but restricted it to more local events, including Stirling Moss's controversial win at Aintree in front of Juan-Manuel Fangio in 1955 in the Mercedes Grand Prix car. Consequently, I missed the tragic 1955 Le Mans won by Mike Hawthorn and Ivor Bueb in the Jaguar D-Type and also the Jaguar victories in 1956 and 1957. The 1950s was, in my opinion, the greatest decade of motor racing in history, when all the leading Formula One drivers competed in sports car racing as well. I feel privileged to have witnessed it.

My next visit to Le Mans was in 1959 with another good friend, Alex Bullen, when we travelled in luxury in his Sunbeam Talbot which, unfortunately, was to 'blow up' on the motorway coming home. We were only doing approximately ninety mph at the time (honestly m'lud) and arrived home late by train. Although there were no Jaguars to support, as it was an Aston Martin benefit, we had an interesting experience which only cosmopolitan Le Mans can provide. This time we booked a Grand Comfort tent with in-built bed frames and it was whilst cooking our usual English breakfast outside on our portable stove that the aroma of frying bacon and eggs attracted much attention. First we had a visit from an attractive young girl who appeared to be a 'camp follower' as we had noted her garments (knickers) strewn over the guy ropes of more than one tent over the weekend! However, we only offered her delicious bacon an eggs (honestly m'lud) and our next visitors were even more interesting.

Two men arrived in a Citroën Safari estate car and beckoned us over to the open rear door. Laid out on the floor were several steel boxes. Sliding the lid off one box, it contained a writhing mass of snakes. Choosing one, he handed it to me advising me not to worry as it was not poisonous and was not an indigenous breed to France, but originated in Persia in the days when monarchs gave gifts to each other during a visit. By this time, a crowd had gathered and as is it slithered up and down my bare arm and its head with its probing tongue reached the inside of my wrist he snatched it away. Lesson: 'Never let a stranger give you a brightly coloured snake without being introduced'. He invited us to his private zoo, but we declined as we had to get home as soon as the race finished.

One of the cars entered was by Ted Lund, an MGA which he was sharing the driving with Colin Escott. I knew Colin because his family had a business in Shudehill Market in Manchester not far from my work place and would meet him now and again. We were in the pits during practice on the Friday evening when the MGA with Colin driving arrived abruptly to a stop with the front of the car smashed in. He had hit an Alsatian dog on the Mulsanne straight when he must have been doing 130 mph. Needless to say the dog did not survive and Colin was very shaken. There were enough hazards on the Le Mans circuit without such incidents although in my experience the officials did remarkably well to keep the track clear.

The following year I witnessed a competition launch of the Jaguar E-Type at Oulton Park when Graham Hill won with Roy Salvadori third, but I was not interested at the time in the new rear and mid-engine Grand Prix cars. I had seen the great front engine models, i.e. Alfa Romeo type 158, Ferrari 4.5-litre unblown, Maserati 250 FF, Ferrari Dino and Vanwall, and with the demise of the Jaguar D-Type and Lister Jaguar my interest waned for both Formula One and sports car racing, although I continued to attend the more important events.

In 1973, my own company and Ascot Caravan Company Limited were thriving so I decided to buy a high performance sports car. Wilmslow Motors in Cheshire was the local distributor for Jensen and I arranged a test drive in their latest model, the Jensen 541 with V8 Chrysler engine. It was very powerful, but I was not impressed with the ride, surprisingly very bumpy. They had a second hand 1972 series III Jaguar E-Type 2+2 Coupe in the showroom with 10,000 miles on the clock. After a trial run, I bought the car and so began a thirty-four-year ownership which involved many thousands of miles on continental tours and holidays abroad, trips to Scotland and Ireland. Four years later in 1977 I was to have the car race prepared and so began a fifteen-year career of club circuit racing, sprints and hill climbs.

1972 Jaguar Series III E-Type 2+2 coupe, Reg. No. HTU 942K photographed in 1973 and owned for 34 years. Race prepared in 1977.

CHAPTER 11

Holidays in Florida

After the debacle of the collapse of Ascot Caravans Ltd, Ascot Caravan (Exports) Ltd and Ascot Caravans International SA through no fault of our own and the lack of managerial control in Arleigh whilst I was away on other business, John Burnell, who was ostensibly the general manager, in fact acted in an office manager capacity only as he had been at Leason. I employed Roy Hines as the overall manager to make sure the company was run efficiently and without further conspiracies. This trust was not fulfilled.

So later in September 1978, after this traumatic business period, we booked a holiday in Florida and hired a car, driving down to the Florida Keys where we rented an apartment. First we called on my brother-in-law, Sheila's youngest sibling, Peter Slater. Peter worked on Tartan Farms, a famous race horse company, and he was responsible for transporting these racehorses to meetings like the Kentucky Derby when he carried a pump-action shotgun to deter prospective criminals from stealing his valuable cargo.

We were to go again in October/November 1981 and visited the Daytona Speedway 500 to support fellow Lancastrian Brian Redman, who was driving a Lola T600 racecar. He told me later that he lifted his foot off the accelerator in the last few hundred yards which allowed John Paul Junior in a Porsche 935 to 'pip him at the post'. However, although disappointed he had in fact clinched the Camel GT Championship for that reason.

1981 Florida Daytona Speedway 500 with Brian Redman's Lola T600 on pole

Brian relaxing after qualifying Lola T600. Chief mechanic John Bright was to become a successful race driver himself.

Whilst in Florida we visited a 'street rod' show in Daytona Beach with a fantastic range of amateur-built specials, but our greatest surprise was to be invited by Walter Hill, the doyen of American Jaguar classic car collectors at that time, to his museum situated on a 55,000 acre ranch near Fort Lauderdale to view his unique collection of Jaguars. In this hangar he had two classic aeroplanes reminding him of his life as an Eastern Airline pilot in his younger days.

It was some eleven years later, in 1992, when we visited Peter again, now with his wife, Murl, at his new address at Quail Roost Farm, where he was responsible for the agricultural side and racehorse transport. He also had the job of keeping the water moccasins under control by shooting them around the farm lake. A very dangerous snake. The owner of the farm bred 'Zeedonks', which are a cross between a donkey and a zebra. In appearance they were similar to a normal donkey but with stripes! The female of the species was not enamoured of their wild consorts and would try to run a mile to escape! However, all Zeedonks are born sterile so it was not an ongoing problem.

One of the exceptional hot rods at the Street Rod Show in Daytona - 1981

During a celebratory dinner all four of us were drinking to excess, particularly myself as I had been sent a bottle of clear alcohol from their illicit still by Murl's parents in Georgia labelled 'For Ron'.

There was a fear amongst the white population living near Miami, one of the worst crime cities in the USA, that the black majority would rise up and attack them, which is why many white people in the outskirts were heavily armed. Whilst

Zeedonks grazing in a field at Quail Roost Farm, Ocala, Florida

Sheila and brother Peter Slater in Florida

discussing this, Peter asked Murl to show us his armoury and she went to the bedroom to fetch a plastic bag containing several handguns, all of them kept loaded for immediate use, including a .45 Magnum. Peter asked Murl to show me her personal revolver of .38 calibre. Handing it to me, she did not know that the safety catch was not locked on. At the last moment, due I believe to my ingrained army training, I did not aim it at anyone present and the hair trigger sent the bullet through the wall of the wooden bungalow. This near tragedy is still recorded by the hole right through the wall to this day. The frivolity quickly ended.

We visited Peter and Murl again in 1994 after Peter had been taken ill with cancer. I managed to persuade his specialist to let him come home where he was regularly visited by Macmillan nurses. During this sad period I took the opportunity to fly up to Newark Valley in New York State and visit my American cousins for a few days. I stayed with cousin Dorothy and called at the farm where I had lived in 1949 with my Uncle Bill and Auntie Bernice and which was now run by their son, young Billy.

The farm was much bigger than I remembered it, with the latest technology including a computer in the milking parlour and a mound of white cotton seed buds outside which was cheap, high protein feed for the Holstein dairy cattle. Dairy farmers in the UK struggle to make a living, especially with the supermarkets not paying a fair price but the same situation applies in the USA.

Peter's racehorse transporter with a capacity of up to 12 racehorses, 54' x 8' wide

My eldest American cousin, Lillian's son Jeffrey, was an enthusiast for American supercars and I was allowed a drive in his Chevrolet Camaro Z28 which had a lot of power but its handling was limited on the local country roads.

We returned again to Florida in 1995 when Peter was given only a few weeks to live and died whilst we were there at the age of fifty-seven years. After the funeral, we returned home to scatter his ashes at his favourite 'playground' as a boy, by the stream at the end of his parents' family home in Poynton, Cheshire.

The Needham farm greatly expanded since the author's first visit in 1949

Lillian's son Jeff shows Ron one of his Camaro Z28 supercars

Ron has a run in another of Jeff's supercars. 1981 Z28 Camaro - October 1995

The cousins discuss the future prospects

Ron and young Billy discuss the advantage of high protein cotton seed feed to high yielding Holstein dairy cows - October 1995

Sheila stands with Walter Hill by a Jaguar XKSS in Walter's museum

Superlative lightweight Jaguar E-Type, allegedly CUT 7

Fastest D-Type Jaguar recorded 2-way, 188 mph at Bonneville salt flats - Walter Hill's museum

CHAPTER 12

Overseas Tours

In 1981 my wife and I joined the Jaguar Drivers' Club trip to Geneva to celebrate the twentieth anniversary of the launch of the E-Type in Switzerland. It was decided by the club officials that the cars should travel in convoy, divided into groups and the leaders of each group were given walkie-talkie radios to keep in touch with each other. Although I was asked to lead the older cars, I was not given a radio and my group included a rusty old 3.5-litre Jaguar saloon. In arranging this the organisers must have thought I would not be able to charge off in my race-prepared car (some hope!).

This convoy was supposed to travel sedately (sixty mph) behind the group led by George Gibbs, the current Chairman of the E-Type register. I soon got fed up with this sedate pace which was going nowhere and on one straight bit of the route nationale I brought my group, which was at the rear of the other groups, into the middle of the road and gradually overtook the others at just a few mph faster, without any acknowledgement by any of the drivers or passengers. It was a hilarious scene and could have been taken out of an episode by John Cleese in *Fawlty Towers*! In spite of this I was congratulated for the way I had kept our group together.

It was in March 1984 that Jaguar Ltd invited Sheila and me, with David and Helga Harvey (former JDC chairman) and John and Rose Owen (current JDC chairman) to join them on the flight to Monza to see the 500 kilometre race for the European Touring Car Championship, which Tom Walkinshaw won. On the return flight I was able to interview Win Percy, who was one of the successful team drivers, for the *Jaguar Driver* magazine.

GENEVA 81

Jaguar Drivers' Club
Commemorative Rally
England to Switzerland
This Certificate was awarded to
R. Lea
Who drove to Geneva Switzerland in one of the 90 Jaguars taking part in the rally Commemorating the 20th Anniversary of the launch of the Jaguar 'E' Type.
6TH JUNE - 13TH JUNE 1981
Vehicle E Type
Registration Number HTU 942K

Sir William Lyons
Chairman Jaguar Cars Ltd
1961

John Egan
Chairman Jaguar Cars Ltd
1981

Certificate for 1981 Commemorative Rally to Geneva

Prior to this I had been invited by Hugo Tippett, one of the TWR team, to visit the TWR works in Kidlington where I met Tom Walkinshaw for the first time. I was interested to see the outboard brake system which they had managed to persuade the organisers of the European Touring Car Championship to accept instead of the production car inboard, rear brake system, which caused serious overheating to the rear brake calipers and the differential of my race-prepared V12 E-Type. I asked Tom how much the conversion cost, which he advised was £10,000.00. This was in the early eighties and hardly a proposition for an amateur driven race car in club motorsport.

Sheila, David Harvey, Helga Harvey, Rose and John Owen enjoy the race of Monza, 1984, courtesy Jaguar Cars Ltd

All three TWR Jaguar XJS V12's at the front of the grid, Monza, 1984

The 1981 rally to Switzerland had been so enjoyable that the twenty-five-year commemorative event this year was eagerly anticipated by my wife, Sheila, and myself. The only reservation I had was that the car was even more race-prepared on this occasion. The Intermarque Challenge Championship gets more competitive every year and in addition, following an oil surge at JDC Mallory Park, the engine had to be completely rebuilt and there was no time to run it in beforehand.

Whilst the car is used regularly on the road in the summer, this was a *tour de force* for a highly tuned race engine. The only concession to the car's new role was a high 2.88:1 axle ratio to improve the normal 6–8 mpg racing fuel consumption; the standard 205VR 70 × 15 Dunlop textile radials, which hopefully would soften the ride of the stiffened suspension; and the original 'tatty' carpets to deaden the clatter synonymous with racing sports cars. Incidentally, the high axle ratio also gave the car a very high top speed which, with the assistance of the aerodynamic fibreglass bonnet, must have been in the region of 160 mph. The straight through exhaust system was silenced by

Tom Walkinshaw (TWR) acknowledges the plaudits after winning the race

Ready for the start. Untimed hillclimb - Geneva Commemorative Rally - 1981

A racing start which was to end in tears? Hit a kerb stone and damaged a wheel.

A gathering of Jaguar E-Types on 25th anniversary tour to Geneva, 1986

two Series I tail pipes and was very noisy but acceptable over seventy or eight mph, when the noise was left behind. It was to become tiresome after long periods in convoy, however.

The St John Horsfall race meeting at Silverstone on 21st June was the start of rally for us; the sixth round of the Intermarque was the draw, but this time not as a competitor. The thought of racing and risking the car just thirty-six hours before leaving for France was too much for even this keen supporter of the Series. The JDC team gained a very satisfactory result, retaining the lead over the Porsche team.

We had a leisurely run down from London to Brighton the next day for the E-Type Day and to meet some of our companions on the rally and then on to the motel at Dover in the evening. Leaving the ferry at Calais early the next day we were initially in convoy with three series III models. The Périphérique in Paris was safely negotiated without too much trauma and we were on the autoroute heading for the first overnight stop at Dijon.

Black clouds ahead heralded a thunderstorm and when it arrived it was something to remember. Not having any heating or demisting system, the windscreen was quickly 'fogged up' and only the strenuous efforts of the 'little woman', wiping the same frantically, enabled reasonable progress. No contact at this stage with any continental Jaguar clubs, the French members apparently keeping to themselves and it was not until the second day when we arrived at the Swiss border at La Cure that our friends from the Jaguar Club Genève greeted us with very welcome refreshments. Taken in convoy down to the hotel at Chavannes de Bogis, this seemed to be the real start of the rally, as all the cars parked together and were a truly magnificent sight.

It was on the road from Dijon that a badly vibrating front wheel necessitated a stop but nothing particularly untoward was found and it was only some time later when it recurred did the cause become clear, a sticking nearside front brake

1986 Switzerland Tour to Geneva
Ron's race prepared E-Type on the Quay

caliper, together with very hard new DS11 racing pads, the remedy for which was a sharp tap on the brake pedal. No doubt the servo was faulty but it could wait until our return home.

The plan for the first official day was a journey in convoy through the old part of Geneva which would have been pleasant in normal circumstances but with the temperature in the high eighties, stop-start roadworks along the way, together with the 'in or out' racing clutch, both the driver and the engine became overheated and we were glad of the respite to fill up the depleted header tanks (two on this car) from one of the many fountains in the historic part of the city.

As usual, Eric Biass, the ever-attentive Geneva club secretary, remained on hand to lead us up Mont Salève where the hang gliding had been arranged. Racing ahead in his Series 1 XJ6, Eric really pushed his car up the winding road with its traditional hairpin bends. With little power below 3000 rpm, I was finding first gear necessary to keep up with him. Further thrills were in store at the top of this 1500 metre mountain, the promised hang-gliding.

Ron hang-gliding with instructor,
1986 JDC Geneva Tour

No details of this event had been given so with some trepidation I watched Philippe Bernard, the boss of the hang-gliding school, assemble the first glider from parts in a valise! After checking that the camera attached to the glider frame was working, essential to record the 'fear' of the novice in flight, a brief demonstration was given to yours truly on how one should run alongside him towards the abyss hanging on his harness straps. I was relieved to find I had a harness as well. At this point, my confidence was further eroded when my wife suggested that I had better give her the car keys before I jumped!

Whilst organiser Tony Dudmesh recited my obituary the intrepid birdman and his apprentice awaited the right conditions to take off. This involved something akin to a three-legged race down a slatted wooden runway to the 4500 foot drop. This was the moment of truth and down we ran and up, soaring into the sky as the updraught from the cliff caught the wings. From thereon it was an unforgettable experience turning into the wind and 'hanging' in a clear blue sky before zooming down and round again. The altitude was brought home to me when I spotted a light aircraft below flying along the valley. It was an exhilarating fifteen minutes before landing in a field at the bottom. Several members took the opportunity to have a go, a moment to savour.

Brian Wilkinson and partner Mary with Sheila taking cover during the stifling heat on the Interlaken airfield. Geneva tour, 1986

It was following this trip to the top of the mountain that the starter motor packed up, a combination no doubt of excessive heat whilst racing, particularly in view of its location close to the exhaust manifold, and the cotton windings usual in these early starters. From now on it was necessary to become somewhat circumspect when parking, but even in this Alpine country, slopes were not always just to hand and I was grateful for the push-start assistance from our friends, Brian Wilkinson and Mary, on more than one occasion. Brian had a Series II 2+2 coupe to exactly the same specifications as my car when I bought it in 1973, even down to the colour. There were times when we envied the quietness and comfort of the standard car.

Photograph taken by Dr Urs Graf of Ron demonstrating his race prepared E-Type at speed (140 mph) on Swiss motorway

It was this starting problem together with extremely hot conditions at altitude on the climb up to the Lötschberg Tunnel that made a 'clear run' essential if I wasn't to block the road; many apologies to members waiting patiently when I jumped the queue. It was here that the cars were driven on to the car-carrying railway wagons and carried under the mountain to be greeted by our next hosts, the Jaguar Drivers' Club of Switzerland. Dr Urs Graf volunteered to take us and Michael and Dianne Harwood, who had clutch problems on their E-Type, down to the Jaguar agent in Interlaken whilst the rest of the contingent were taken to the airfield outside the town to be parked overnight, the venue of the official driving tests and concours.

A mildly race modified Jaguar E-Type with a fully modified wife. Geneva, 1986

The proprietor of the garage, Holk Oertler-Balmer, went out of his way to help us and Urs obtained a second-hand starter from a contact near his home in Zurich and delivered it to the garage. Not only was the car soon fully mobile through their combined efforts, but Dr Graf was able to prescribe antibiotics from his army medical bag to clear up my throat infection. Even surgeons have to do their annual army service in Switzerland. Whilst the official itinerary was being carried out at the airfield, a high speed demonstration run up the motorway was some small return for his kindness and help although we could not find any Porsche to play with. It was a relief to get the problem sorted out.

Holk Oertler-Balmer, the Jaguar agent, asked me if I could employ his son, Christian, in our transport/motor racing garage for a short period so that he could learn more about Jaguars and improve his English. In due course he arrived at Compstall Mills and stayed with Tim, our youngest son.

Leaving Interlaken we cruised noisily through the eleven miles of the St Gothard tunnel to enjoy the hospitality of the Swiss Jaguar E-Type Club at Brunnen on Lake Lucerne. Leaving this idyllic place on Friday 4th July, the two red E-Types headed for the Schlumpf Museum at Mulhouse. Arriving at the main entrance, the enthusiastic staff opened the main gates to the VIP car park, such is the charisma of the E-Type! Gathering around the car, bonnet up, questions and answers in a mixture of pidgin English and broken French, they were keen to know the specification and how fast it would go; 'formidable' was the more general comment.

E-Types on display outside the Hotel Brunnen, 1986 Geneva tour

It was on the return journey that I had a high speed rear tyre tread separation, which could have resulted in a bad accident when on the motorway. The wheels on the E-Type were fitted with Michelin TB15 tyres for racing but whilst allegedly road legal were hardly suitable for a long tour on continental roads. However, I still retained the original 205 × 70 × 15 Dunlop tyres supplied when the car was new and as they had substantial tread on them I had them fitted. I did not allow for the deterioration of the rubber compound in dry stock and this was the fundamental reason for the detached tread at speed.

At the time I was the Captain of the JDC team in the Intermarque Challenge Championship between teams of AC Cobras, Aston Martins, Ferraris and Porsche. Coming across a Porsche 911 at some 80 to 90 mph, I proceeded to pass when it speeded-up. At some 130–140 mph I came alongside when there was a loud bang which I assumed was an engine misfire as it was peaking at 6500–7000 rpm at the time. Slackening off, I came again and passed the Porsche who had slowed down. Arriving at the ferry port I checked the car and found that the rear off-side tyre tread had detached from the casing and hit the underside of the rear wing so hard that it lifted a slither of metal/paint. Miraculously the tyre did not deflate. The consequences could have been disastrous but I did not tell Sheila in case she became alarmed and abandoned my 'mistress' (E-Type) and got the train home!!

The final mileage can only be estimated, the high axle ratio meant the milometer was incorrect, but it was certainly more than 2500 miles, possibly 3000. The engine never missed a beat, its remarkable flexibility even in raced tuned guise is not only a tribute to the soundness of its basic design but to the preparation by my racing mechanic, Don Law, and to the expertise of Ron Beaty of Forward Engineering who prepares my engines. The car was taken straight off the racing track and carried two people with all their luggage to complete this memorable event. The engine is nicely run-in now, ready to take part in the last six races of this season.

Ron's E-type leads the convoy of Jaguars round the Nordschleife race crcuit. Black Forest Rally, Germany, 1988

In August 1988 we arrived at Dover docks to take the 5.30 am ferry which left with thirty-five Jaguars, mostly E-Types, for the Black Forest Rally arranged with the Jaguar Association of Germany. The highlight of this trip was the opportunity to visit a motor museum at Schloss Langenburg and in the courtyard of this castle we were able to display our Jaguars in this historic setting. Later we were to visit the Nürburgring and I took a convoy of E-Types round this famous circuit.

In May 1989 we joined the other members on a Scandinavian rally incorporating Denmark, Norway and Sweden in the E-Type. Supported by Castrol it received entries from all over Europe and almost every model that Jaguar cars had ever made. There were

Ron and Sheila park the Jaguar E-Type in the Nürburgring paddock after the trip round the race circuit, 1988

highlights too numerous to mention but the run to Geiranger in Norway was outstanding with a superb sweeping road up to the snow line and then in convoy through the huge snow drifts down to the hotel situated at the end of the sea fiord 500 metres deep! Glad to have four-pot CanAm racing brakes and vented discs front and rear!

It was at the port of Most that my wife and I were entertained at a restaurant by F. R. W. 'Lofty' England and his chauffeur who had been on the rally with us were able to reminisce about the early Le Mans days, but more of this later. Finally, when we returned to Denmark for a banquet and prize-giving I was surprised to be announced as the winner of the booby prize, a lump of Norwegian stone presented for exceeding the minimum time allowance during the speed trials earlier that day at the Jyllandsringen race track with passenger Clive Brandon.

Gathering of Jaguars outside French château. Paladin Jaguar Cognac Rally, 1989

The origins of this stone picked up in Norway were a legend to Danish members and I was given the admonishment to keep it safe and bring it to the Austrian rally in 1991. What better excuse could one wish for to join them in another rally?

Later that year, in September, we were invited by Colin McMeakin and Jim Ross-Tomlin of Paladin Jaguar to join them on the Cognac Rally which had the backing of Martell, the brandy distillers in France, at which we were royally entertained and on the return route took the opportunity to visit Oradour-sur-Glane where the civilian population were massacred by the Nazis in 1944. The village remains as it was when it was destroyed and there is an eerie silence with no birds to be seen and no sound whatsoever.

Sheila stands guard over E-Type-Paladin Jaguar.
Cognac Rally, 1989

A stop for refreshments in Norway
on the Scandinavian Rally, 1989

The backdrop of the Norwegian
landscape. Scandinavian Rally, 1989

Unusual driving conditions in Norway.
Scandinavian rally, 1989

Sheila waits patiently for her chauffer outside the Hotel in Geiranger, Norway

Uwe Kai (The Red Baron) our favourite Austrian E-Type owner. Vienna, 1991

In the next two years I was heavily committed in the removal of my company, Arleigh International, to the Midlands until the Austria-Hungary tour in June 1991. This Rally of Jaguars and their enthusiastic owners was organised by members of the Austrian Jaguar Drivers' Club following the very successful Scandinavian rally of the Jaguar Club of Denmark in 1989. Ready for a leisurely run across Holland and Germany, some nineteen assorted Jaguars assembled at Sheerness on the Isle of Sheppey for the evening departure on the luxurious ferry the *Britannia*, arriving at Vlissingen (Flushing) in Holland at 7.00 am on Tuesday 28th May. Before leaving the UK, the British party, together with the Danish and Luxembourg parties, had received a most generous invitation from our favourite Austrian E-Type owner, 'The Red Baron' and his wife, Uwe and Ursula Kai to join them at a typical Bavarian restaurant at Lake Tegernsee. With much 'bonhomie' the trip was off to a good start. With two overnight stops en route we arrived at Salzburg on 30th May to renew old friendships and make new acquaintances at the Winkler Restaurant with a panoramic view of the ancient city. The following day set the pattern of the trip with lunch at the Frischer lakeside restaurant and welcoming speeches in St Gilgen by the Bergermaster, Mr Panberger. In the evening a bit of culture; a chamber music concert in the Mozarteum which strangely did not include any Mozart in the programme. However, I was pleased to renew my acquaintance with Mr Lofty England who joined my wife and myself for the performance.

Ron and Sheila park the E-Type in Budapest. Austrian Ungarn Tour, 1991

The highlight of the following day was the passage of the Grossglockner Pass over the Alps, the highest pass in Austria, which we were fortunate to see in glorious clear weather, the heat of the sun causing avalanches heard and viewed from a safe distance. Travelling alone or in small passes, the fabulous Alpine scenery was as memorable as the sight and sound of those superb cars winding their way along the excellent roads.

Monday 3rd June was an early departure for the longest day run (303 miles) to the Hotel Club Tihany in Hungary. We received an enthusiastic 'Isten Hozta' (welcome) by the Hungarians who must have been astounded at the sight of these capitalist 'toys' after more than forty years of communism. In fact, one citizen was so overcome he ran into a member's Jaguar XJ12, which was called 'The Skoda Crusher' from thereafter. On the following day we gathered in the hotel car park (all 100-plus cars) for the trip to Budapest with police motorcycle escort. Arriving in Budapest[1], we parked at the Pest side of the river Danube with the higher Buda part of the city across the water. Taken by coach, still with a police escort, we were given a fast trip around the most outstanding features and several decided to stay while others returned for the trip to the speed test venue. Originally, we were supposed to have enjoyed a visit to the Hungaroring racing circuit, scene of the Group A victory for TWR Jaguar XJSs in the past but following well publicised (in racing circles) advertising politics within the Formula 1 circus this was denied us and we had to be satisfied with an abandoned airfield which the organisers had done well to arrange at such short notice. Local villagers gathered to watch these raucous sports cars at 'full chat' in an area where draught horses are still the main source of everyday power for agricultural implements and transport. One particular recollection of this event was a traditional Hungarian local with a large handle-bar moustache directing the traffic from the main road on his own initiative and who was an out of work MiG fighter pilot!

More sedate transport for Sheila and Ron with John and Heather Powers. Vienna, 1991

Ron standing by his Jaguar TWR XJ12 saloon.
JDC Chilterns Tour to Spain, 1994.
(This was the car involved in an accident in 1996.)

Leaving Hungary the following day we arrived at Wien (Vienna) in the afternoon for a well earned rest and relaxation. The gala dinner that evening was a super affair to cap this get together and the Danish couple, Jens and Dorit Jeppesen, were presented with the competition winner's prize of a framed copy

1 This city comprises two parts each side of the River Danube

JDC members and their cars gather outside the hotel. Chiltern's Tour 1994

of Terry Cuneo's painting of Lofty England supervising a pit stop of the winning C-Type (Hamilton and Rolt) at Le Mans. The infamous booby prize held by the writer since the Scandinavian rally, mounted and inscribed 'THE STONE', was presented to the chairman of the Jaguar Drivers' Club of Italy for the temerity to propose that the next rally should be held in Italy in 1993!

In fact, it was in May 1994 that my wife and I took part in the Chilterns area of the Jaguar Drivers' Club to Spain. For the first time, however, we did not tour in the Jaguar E-Type which I bought in 1973 but in a TWR Jaguar XJ12 saloon with the registration number WXJ1. This very comfortable, high performance car had air conditioning which was to be a boon on this trip with the ambient temperature in the nineties. Because Beverley Maxwell and Martin Routledge lived in Spain (Martin was a former Jaguar agent there) they were able to arrange several civic receptions with the Spanish authorities and we were treated to police-escorted tours of ancient cities, i.e. Vittoria, Pensicola, etc. Unfortunately, the car had an alternator problem but fortunately a member had a spare on board and other members fitted it to the engine.

We kept in touch with Martin and Beverley and in February 1996 visited France and Spain with our 32ft Fleetwind Flair American R.V. towing a Renault Clio saloon. We left the motor home in France and travelled down to Spain in the Renault to stay with the Routledge's who entertained us royally. One memorable occasion was an invitation to visit a Leper Colony run by the R.C. church which a leprosy specialist from London visited every week. These victims of this biblical disease were originally locked away behind a high stone wall and forgotten, but were now treated humanely although with their 'Lion' faces were not allowed to mix with the population. Some of them had been French partisans in the War who had lived in the wild and suffered from lack of hygiene and malnutrition eventually suffering from incurable leprosy.

This 5.3-litre XJ production saloon was modified by Tom Walkinshaw Racing (TWR) with a five-speed manual ZF gearbox, tuned suspension and low profile tyres to give a 'Jekyll and Hyde' character which could be driven sedately due to the immense torque of the engine or with a 'burst on the banjo' to give a very fast and good handling large saloon.

It was when travelling from my company in Warwickshire and between Ashbourne and Buxton in Derbyshire late one afternoon, I rounded a blind corner to find a Volvo car was overtaking two cars and a car and caravan and completely blocking my nearside carriageway. Only my motor racing experience avoided a head-on crash at a combined speed of some 120 mph. Immediate reaction was to brake and then within fractions of a second, release same so that the steering was regained and I swerved the car through the adjacent dry stone wall, dropping three or four feet into a grass field and stopping eventually, still on all four wheels although the car had nearly turned over in flight.

Sitting stunned in the driver's seat a person ran up to the car and said, 'I bet you would like to punch me on the jaw.' It was the driver of the Volvo, an Ulsterman who had taken the unbelievable risk of overtaking the traffic before a blind corner and who had clearly not reacted whatsoever as there were no signs of panic braking on the road surface. His guilty reaction in stopping immediately after the near fatal incident and his guilty statement took the wind out of my sails for I did not take up his request by 'thumping' him but berated him in no uncertain terms and told him to clear off. I was told later that some council workers had stopped him. Meanwhile, all the traffic had stopped as I climbed out of the car to inspect the damage, which was extensive.

Soon after, PC Plod arrived on his bicycle but he declined to climb down into the field and I went back up to the road to give him the details, where all the innocent drivers of the overtaken vehicles, including the one towing the caravan, who had children aboard, gathered to congratulate me on my evasive action in an accident which would certainly have involved them. Amazingly, although the Ulsterman's insurance company paid for all the repairs to my car including a personal damage claim, he was not charged by the police. Although I wrote to the Chief Constable expressing my surprise that such dangerous driving was not punished, especially as I had several witnesses, I can only assume that PC Plod's attitude at the scene reflected the police authority's complacent attitude to an accident black spot. They were not able to control dangerous driving so hard luck on the innocent victims.

Racing a heavy sports car, the Jaguar V12 E-Type, I had regular experience of taking evasive action, particularly lifting off the brake to regain steering control and it was this inbuilt reaction which was the saviour on this occasion.

Although the unique Jaguar saloon was a virtual write-off, my only consolation was that behind the dry stone wall there could have been a Derbyshire stone quarry with possible fatal consequences. In fact the XJ12 was repaired by well known Jaguar specialists in the Midlands but I was never happy driving it and eventually sold it and transferred the special number plate to a 4-litre XJS 'Celebration' convertible coupe, WXJ1.

My stroke attack in July 1996 left me unable to cope with a manual gear box. Therefore this race prepared E-Type had to be 'civilised' after twenty-three years' ownership and the car was fitted with an automatic gearbox, air conditioning, cruise control, etc. My wife and I had enjoyed the previous E-Type Anniversary tours and in 2001 the JDC arranged the fortieth. While the journey to Geneva was memorable it was also exhausting because the route took us more than 2000 miles of mainly N and D French roads which must have been equivalent to at

Courtesy of Moët & Chandon the fantastic 40th anniversary cake for the Jaguar E-Type. Switzerland, 2001

least 6000 miles of autoroute over the sixteen days. I was not the only disabled person on the trip; John Hulme managed it with the assistance of his son, Robert. His BRG Series II Roadster had comprehensive hand controls. John had been paralysed from the waist down since a fall from a horse when he was fifteen years old and was wheelchair-bound. We were both gratified to receive a handsome ornament in recognition of our efforts from Eric Biass, President of the Jaguar Club Genève. I was grateful for the assistance of members, particularly from Area 18 Lancashire and old friends from the Chiltern area.

In spite of what I thought was meticulous preparation, my Series III E-Type engine overheated with the ambient temperature at 80°F. Fortunately, our good friends John and Kath Butterworth and John and Elaine Birchall travelled with us and were of invaluable help.

Amongst the highlights of the trip was a party at the Château de Pizay when we were entertained by a French rock and roll band which started with an artiste giving a fantastic rendition of Edith Piaf's songs and continued with wonderful dance rhythms which even had me gyrating in a limited way to the music, and completed by a great sketch with a blonde, nubile wench arriving on the back of a Harley Davidson and stripping to the sensual rhythm. As befits E-Type owners, we were not allowed to see the ultimate eroticism of the 'full monty' in case it jeopardised our ability to continue on the tour the next morning! The Harley Davidson was in concourse condition as well! This was to be the last continental tour in the E-Type Jaguar although it was used regularly in the UK.

Even disabled people can follow the rhythm of a Jazz Band. Château de Pizay, 2001

On 28th May 2004, we visited Spain again, but this time in the 4-litre Jaguar XJS Celebration drop head coupe. Staying again at the Parador hotels we visited the usual towns but did not have the assistance of the expat Brits, Beverley and Martin, who arranged so many meetings and events with local authorities. It was extremely hot again, so much so that sometimes we had to raise the power hood to protect ourselves from the sun!

The following year we took this car for a brief holiday with the XJ Register when we visited the Rheims racing circuit, following which we had short holidays in the Republic of Ireland arranged by the Jaguar Enthusiasts' Club when our friends, John and Kath Butterworth, took us sightseeing in their Jaguar Mark IX saloon and we parked our own car at the hotel.

Although a 'disabled pedestrian', I was *not* a 'disabled driver' but the stress of wear and tear since my stroke more than ten years previously was beginning to take effect on my mobility and I was using a battery-powered buggy more and more often.

Oh La La! Hospitalité Français at the Château de Pizay. Geneva Tour, 2001

High speed convoy in France. Geneva Tour, 2001

Jaguar XJS Celebration convertible used to tour Spain in 2004 and France (Rheims) 2005.
Note Reg. No transferred from TWR Jaguar saloon.

CHAPTER 13

Entry into Motorsport

In 1973 I bought a 1972 Series III Jaguar E-Type 2+2 coupe and in 1977, at the twenty-first anniversary meeting of the Jaguar Drivers' Club at Donington Park, I entered this completely standard car with three-speed BorgWarner automatic gearbox in the Modified/Production race. It was won by Richard Gamble in a fully modified racing E-Type roadster, a car I was to buy from him later. I finished fifth overall in this race with my 'bog standard' road-going car. I was forty-six years old at the time and it awakened my enthusiasm for motor racing but this time as a competitor.

The car needed to be race-prepared and although the heavy Series III E-Type with its V12 engine was not generally raced, I took it to Terry Moore of Phoenix Engineering in Goole, East Yorkshire for this work. He first asked me to take him for a run in the car along local roads so that he could assess if I had the ability to handle this powerful car and make his race preparation and support worthwhile. He agreed to work on the car and it was left with him.

The automatic gearbox was replaced with a four-speed manual box, a 3.77:1 differential and the standard wheels were fitted with new Michelin XWX tyres. As the intention was to race in the production class very little modification was allowed under the rules so that the power steering had to be retained which was far too light for racing. It was essential, however, to do something about the brakes, particularly the rears which were inboard and overheated at racing speeds. An angled deflector plate was fitted ahead of the calipers to deflect cool air on to same and a hole was cut out of the rear bulkhead to allow the excessive heat to dissipate via an aluminium tube exiting behind the rear number plate.

Braking was always a problem with this very heavy sports car (more than 3446 lbs/1563 kg). The only modification was to the foot controls, with the rubber pads removed and the accelerator pedal extended to facilitate 'heel and toe' gear changing. When I took this car to Silverstone for track testing, which was satisfactorily completed, Terry Moore told me afterwards that his two partners in another business, Paul Skilleter and Phillip Porter, had told him that they did not expect this rather aged driver to lap the old club circuit in under 1 min 20 secs. In fact, my best lap was 1 min 12 secs which pleased Terry and myself. The quickest ever lap time of the old club circuit in a Jaguar was by John 'plastic' Pearson in his GRP bodied XK120, a heavily modified race car, in 59.6 secs.

My first race was in the BRDC Production Sports Car race at Donington Park on 11th September 1977 when I came fifth. Only seven days later I raced at Snetterton in the BRSCC Certina Watch event and came fourth. It was at this event when Terry Moore was present that he instructed his mechanic to wipe clean and then dry the soles of my racing shoes after I had entered the cockpit to make sure they did not slip on the metal pedals. It was this attention to detail which gave a race driver confidence and Terry was very thorough in this respect.

I soon realised after these first two races that the standard production Series III E-Type was not going to be competitive unless it was heavily modified. This was a dilemma because I wished to retain it as a fast touring car and go on continental trips and tours. In addition, the basic car did not lend itself to race modification. The wheelbase had been increased by the factory over the Series I and II models and although the track was increased it was insufficient to compensate for the high polar movement of inertia which in practice meant that when racing and the car got sideways, the normal correction resulted in the car 'whipping round' the other way. The light power steering which could not be removed under production racing rules did not help to control this phenomenon. Therefore, handling was always difficult on slow or medium fast corners, which was the case on most club circuits but much better on grand prix circuits with their very fast bends. These factors of excessive weight and unpredictable handling were the main reasons the Series III was not raced generally. It made a fine Gran Turismo car, however, as was to be proved in the future.

Over the winter of 1977/78 I bought the fully modified E-Type roadster from Richard Gamble. My first race with this car was at Silverstone in March 1978 when I lapped the old club circuit in 65.9 secs which was competitive, but I did not finish. The next event was at Croft where I was second in class and then won the class at Oulton Park and received a cheque for £25.00. A money award was always gratefully received but it was a 'drop in the ocean' compared to the costs of entering and maintaining even a club racing car and I always preferred trophies.

These races were in the STP Modified Sports Car Championship and in the Donington Park round in June I was third behind a 3-litre Marcos which was originally owned and raced by Jonathan Palmer to win the BRSCC Sports Car Championship. A 2.8-litre Porsche Carrera was second. Only seven days later I was first in class at Thruxton in the pouring rain; the first and only time I raced at this circuit. At this period I was third in the STP championship and learning how to cope with this very quick car on slick tyres. At the next event at Croft again I suffered a blow-out on the rear off-side tyre which sent me spinning into the bank at high speed. Fortunately, this E-Type had a steel rear end (unlike the 310WK which had a GRP rear end) which absorbed the impact and so saved me from serious injury but the car was a complete write-off.

First modified E-Type at Thruxton. This car was crashed and a write-off at Croft

This blow-out was caused by the disintegration of the engine of another car I was about to lap. The young driver of this Davrian sports car with Hillman Imp engine was, I was told later, using 12,000 rpm which was the absolute maximum where the engine had been fitted with a Carter steel crankshaft for racing. His engine had a standard crankshaft so that not surprisingly it exploded and left pieces all over the track. This example highlights the hazards of circuit racing compared to sprints or hill-climbs when any accident is one's own error.

So it was back to the V12 E-Type for the rest of the season and I entered my first hill-climb at Loton Park which is located in beautiful countryside near Shrewsbury. It was an enjoyable and less intense occasion but the car was too heavy for a competitive time. In August I was at Silverstone in a mixed marque event and came eighth overall. I was back there in September but this time on the full Grand Prix circuit which suited that car better with a best lap in 2 min 1.85 secs but on the sixth lap I crashed into the catch fencing at Woodcote corner. Later that month I was fifth in class at Donington Park.

Jaguar E-Type into catch fencing on Silverstone Grand Prix circuit

In the following year, in 1979, I competed in seven championship races. Six in the Lucas CAV Production Sports Car Championship and one in the InterMarque in which I did not finish. Races at Snetterton, Oulton Park, Castle Coombe, Mallory Park, Aintree and Donington.

The Intermarque Challenge Championship was a team event between the organising club, Aston Martin Owners' Club, the AC Cobra Club, the Porsche Owners' Club, the Ferrari Owners' Club and the Jaguar Drivers' Club. Twenty points in each race were awarded for first place, down to one point for twentieth. Only Class A standard production cars received maximum points. Class B modified cars received three-quarter points, Class C fully modified cars received half points. In my experience, no standard production car ever won overall and therefore twenty points but I did manage an overall second place in the wet at Donington one year when all the modified cars on slick tyres were caught out by a sudden downpour on the grid. I remember passing Dave Ellis (fully modified Aston) so closely down the Cramer Curves that we touched and left me with yellow paint on my red car at the end of the race.

Silverstone 1983, fierce battle at Copse Corner between Jaguar E-Type and Aston Martin DB3 Intermarque. Photographer D. Parker

It was in the CAV races that I was first in Class at Cadwell Park, fourth overall at Aintree and finished in all the other races against very competitive opposition, including Charles Morgan (Morgan Plus 8), Colin Blower (TVR) on very twisty circuits where the V12 E-Type was at a disadvantage. The photograph shows an incident at Cadwell Park in practice when the brakes 'locked up' and I was determined to miss the Armco barrier but did not realise there was a steep drop out of sight. I was left balancing on the edge with the car 'see-sawing'. I gingerly vacated the car as it was about to fall. The breakdown truck arrived just in time.

In the following year I was not as active because of business pressures and was third overall at Aintree in the CAV Production race in May and then fourth in class at Oulton Park in the Lancashire and Cheshire sprint, first in class at the Goodwood sprint and finally second in class at the Production Jaguar race at Mallory Park in October.

A team of four E-Types and one XK were entered in the Birkett six-hour relay race at the end of the year but only the four E-Types started and one was to retire early which put considerable strain on those left. The inboard disc brakes on my V12 E-Type were so affected by the heat transfer that the oil in the differential started to boil and the fluid dropped on to the ground and 'sizzled' away. It was a testament to the strength of the Powerlok back axle that it did not seize up. For the 1981 season I had the support of Ron Beaty of Forward Engineering but the car had very little modification other than the essential brake cooling attempts by Phoenix Engineering originally. However, the standard front calipers were replaced by the four pot Girling CanAm brakes from the crashed

Jaguar E-type

This season, the venerable E type Jaguar really didn't stand a chance. Placed in Class A of the prodsports championships, it was up against the Morgan V8s and the TVR 3-litres and its unpredictable handling kept it away from the leaders.

Two or three examples were seen during the year, however, most of them boasting the 5.3-litre V12 engine which still powers (albeit in somewhat changed form) the XJS and XJ12 saloons.

A very heavy car, despite it's immense power output, it was at a considerable disadvantage when the very light weight of the two-seater Morgan and the fibre-glass TVR is taken into consideration.

It is still an immensely quick car in straight line, however, and on the longer circuits could just about hold its own. A very enthusiastically conducted example finished well up in the first ever production car 100-mile race at Snetterton early in the year.

Autosport *review of 1978*

The 'achilles heel' of the heavy Series III E-Type. Brakes locked up. Photographer Roger C. Standish

modified E-Type and an air dam from an MGB was fitted at the front. This was to eliminate under steer, always the bugbear of heavy front end Jaguars, but it was soon taken off because it shrouded the front brakes and they overheated.

The Garelli Production Sports Car Championship had taken over the CAV Championship for this season with the same mixture of competitive cars. At the JDC Spring meeting at Silverstone, I was third overall in the production race, fifth in class in the Intermarque and after several good class positions in the Garelli was second in class at the Curborough Sprint.

Birkett Six-Hour Relay at Silverstone. Ron Lea about to pass a Triumph, 1980

Ron's E-Type balancing on the edge, Cadwell Park

The breakdown lorry arrives just in time!

CHAPTER 14

Organising the Cheshire Cats

Early in 1982, at one of the regular monthly meetings of the Jaguar Drivers' Club Area 15 at the Kilton Inn in Mere, Cheshire, the Committee Secretary, Mrs Penny Forsyth, advised that the MAC (Midland Auto Club) had cancelled the race meeting at Oulton Park, Saturday 24th April, and the owners had offered it to us. The area representative, Paul Fell, and myself were keen to take this opportunity if possible and it was decided to ask the board of directors and the competition committee of the JDC for their support. Unfortunately, this was not forthcoming because it was advised they had too much motor racing to organise at the time, the Silverstone meeting being the first historic meeting each year in April. However, I thought this was too good an opportunity to miss and at the next committee meeting we decided to organise the event on our own. I was chairman of the organising committee but first we had to arrange the funding which was done by means of a loan on promissory notes by the committee members.

Paul Fell, Chairman of JDC Area 15 'The Cheshire Cats' with his partner Terry and Sheila

A race meeting cannot be organised without a clerk of the course. Being a member of the BRSCC (British Racing Sports Car Club) I knew some of the officials. I therefore contacted the chairman, Tom Dooley, and asked him if he could recommend an official to be clerk of the course for our meeting. He suggested Mr T. H. Rowe (Tom Rowe) and later contacted him and he agreed to take up this position. Although Tom had been the Transport Manager of the race car team owned by Jack Broadhead, driver Bob Berry in the 1950s, he had not been involved in Jaguar racing for many years and in fact was not to become a member of the Jaguar Drivers' Club until later when Area 15 Committee paid his subscription. It would mean a tremendous effort by all concerned to get the event off the ground and we were likely to lose all the loan money. However, we pressed on with the organisation and I wrote the programme introduction.

We had the help of the Oulton Park officials and of course the usual race marshals but all the committee and staff at Area 15 gave up their weekend to organise the supporting events to the motor races, including Paul Fell, the area representative, secretary Penny Forsyth, David Hough, events organiser, Dave Archer general dogsbody and last but not least Eddie and Joan Farrel who organised the concourse competition, always popular amongst Jaguar car collectors. As the only person with any motor racing experience, I was elected chairman and Sheila, my wife, secretary of the administration for this Cheshire Cats Day.

When I started racing in the late 1970s I competed in a long distance (100 miles) sports car race organised by the BRSCC at Oulton Park and found it to be much more satisfactory than the short sprint races of ten or fifteen laps. I therefore decided that we would have a long distance sports car race at our first meeting which was to be known as the Cheshire Cats Trophy race. This was the third race in the meeting and had fourteen entries; I drove my Jaguar E-Type V12 but did not finish. There were just four races at this event with just a total of thirty-four entries.

Publicity photograph to obtain sponsorship, Ron with ex Warren Pearce fully modified E-Type, 310 WK with racing mechanic Ron Needham.

After a reasonably successful 1981 season with my road going E-Type I still had the ambition to drive a car which could win overall and not just in the class. Over the winter of 1981/82 I bought the famous ex-Warren Pearce fully modified E-Type, registration number 310 WK from Fred Cliffe. The red modified E-Type I crashed at Croft in 1978, when a tyre was punctured through debris on the track, was my first experience of racing with slick tyres (no tread). Most of the Jaguar Intermarque team were on slicks except my V12 E-Type which ran on Michelin XWX originally, then later on Michelin TB15 or Yokohama tyres latterly, all treaded pattern.

My first race in this car was at Silverstone in the JDC Spring Meeting when I failed to finish in the Intermarque race due to a flat battery (no dynamo or alternator on these modified cars to save weight, always started with a separate slave battery on a trolley). In the modified race later, I was first in class with a best lap of 65.5 seconds.

Modified E-Type racing at Oulton Park the Cheshire Cats Meeting but was to retire with broken throttle cable

Competitive, especially for the first time out in this new car. A few weeks later in April, I was second overall in the modified race at Oulton Park (the first Cheshire Cats Trophy Meeting) and retired in the second race with a broken throttle cable after a 'dice' with Malcolm Hamilton in another modified E-Type roadster. In the next meeting in May, at the same venue, I was second overall in the Intermarque behind Dave Ellis in the profile highly modified Aston Martin V8 and finally at the end of May I was first in class at Curborough Sprint, beating Herb Shepherd (the King of Curborough) into second place.

However, at the meeting at Aintree in June, after the practice session, I was to crash this car very badly at Beechers Brook Corner on the first lap. The circumstances of this accident were interesting in that an outside influence caused it. There had been a severe winter that year with the result that frost had permeated the macadam track surface and lifted it in places. As the owner, Mrs Mirabelle Topham, was responsible; on reflection I have since realised that I had a strong case for damages and compensation.

The worst spot was on the apex of Beechers Brook corner (the track follows the horseracing course) and the field did two warm-up laps before the race started, when the marshals at this corner stood on the track pointing warning flags at the hole in the surface. I made a bad start to the race and was in a hurry to catch up. Approaching Beechers corner too fast, I could not take the best line inside the hole at the apex and had to take a wider line to avoid it which took me onto the wet grass on the outside. Slick tyres on wet grass and I was a 'passenger'

The two modified E-Types nose to tail, Cheshire Cats, Oulton, 1982

Ron Lea V12 E-Type catches the original D-Type of David Duffy and John Pearson, Silverstone

and could not take avoiding action as I slid between the two horse racing hedges and hit the outside perimeter concrete fence. The impact took place in the centre of the driver's side and I received a compound fracture of my right forearm. It was the worst accident I ever had whilst racing but I was protected from serious injury by the strength of the monocoque of the E-Type at this point. If I had been in a space frame chassis car I could have been fatally injured.

The car was a virtual write-off and was rebuilt by John Oxborough in 1992 for hill climbing.

It was at the end of 1982 that I received a letter from the Competition Chairman of the JDC referring to the Oulton Park Meeting scheduled for April 1983. A special meeting was called for 1st December 1982 by the committee of Area 15 to discuss the ramifications of the contents of this letter. The main club wished the Oulton Park meeting to become a fixture in the JDC calendar although it was expected that Area 15 members should do all the organising and spadework. A general discussion followed in which the implications of allowing the Oulton Park meeting to be taken over by the main club, or conversely the implications of disregarding the main club's claim to have control. A unanimous decision was taken, in spite of these possible consequences, to reaffirm the decision to go ahead as planned with Area 15 organising the meeting.

The committee had been bitterly disappointed that the main club could not offer any assistance whatsoever the previous year when this racing date had been offered to us.

Following the crash of the modified E-Type 310 WK at Aintree, it was back to the production V12 E-Type for the coming season which commenced with the British Racing Marshals' Club Meeting at Silverstone in March. Most regular club racers supported the marshals' event in recognition of their unpaid support for amateur club racing.

John Pearson (D-Type) and Ron Lea (V12 E-Type) in a close dice

The Davrian leads the field down to Old Hall Corner. Cheshire Cats Meeting

Next was the JDC Spring Meeting at Silverstone in early April in which I was third in the E-Type Historic Race after a close dice with John Pearson and David Duffy in their original D-Types. I was second in class to the overall winner, Roger Mac in the European GT Championship winning E-Type. John Pearson was to become a very good friend later in the promotion of the England/Hawthorn Memorial Appeal. I was third in class in the Intermarque at this meeting.

I was chairman of the organising committee again for the second Cheshire Cats Trophy meeting on 23rd April which was St George's Day and wrote the introduction to the meeting.

In keeping with our policy to present varied entertainment and not just motor racing, we invited the Sealed Knot Society and Morris Dancing teams together with the most ambitious innovation, the tractor pullers. This had been arranged by Ron Beaty who supplied some of the competitors with his engines.

We were also pleased to host the second round of the Robin Hamilton InterMarque Challenge Championship and finally the very popular Cheshire Cats Trophy Race which this year had a mandatory pit stop with a change of drivers if desired. There were a total of ninety-four entries in the five events this year, considerably more than the inaugural event. Driving the V12 E-Type, I was third in class in the first race, first in class in the modified race and third overall in the sixty-lap Cheshire Cats Trophy Race. At Donington Park the following month I was third in class in the Intermarque Championship and then fourth in class in the same championship at Silverstone in June.

The 1982 Oulton Park Meeting with the Davrian on pole ahead of Ron's E-Type and Malcolm Hamilton's E-Type

The JDC organised meeting at Snetterton saw an exciting dice between Tim Sisson (Series II E-Type PEE 22) and myself. I led for most of the way only for Tim to pass at the end. We both set the fastest lap. In the Intermarque at this meeting I was third in class again and the JDC Team came fourth in the relay. In August I was the only Jaguar entered in the production car race at Castle Coombe and was first in class. One of the few times I have driven the car to an event; it was usually trailered because if you have an accident and the car becomes unroadworthy it is very expensive to collect it later.

Finally, we came back to Oulton Park in September where I was first in class, sixth overall in the Intermarque and fourth in the allcomers. The most significant race this year as far as Jaguar aficionados were concerned was the four-hour relay at Oulton Park which the JDC team won for the first time.

It was at the end of this very busy season that it was announced that I was to be presented with the prestigious Jaguar Driver of the Year Award for 1983. This award by the Jaguar Cars Limited was open to drivers worldwide who had enhanced the prestige of the Jaguar marque during the year. The commendation from Jaguar Cars to me read as follows:

For the winning by the JDC Team of the Inter-Club Relay Challenge Trophy over three Relays at Oulton Park, Silverstone and Snetterton, the first time it was ever won by a Jaguar Team. For his leadership, for his services to Club Racing and his own skilled and consistent driving, Ron Lea has been declared Jaguar Driver of the Year.

Ron gets sideways in front of Prater (Aston Martin V8) and Drake (Lister) whilst Webb (modified E-Type) takes a wide berth. Intermarque Silverstone, 1984

In 1984 after the usual Spring Meeting at Silverstone in which I did not finish in the Intermarque race, I was fourth in class in the Modified/Historic race. This year the Cheshire Cats Trophy Meeting was held on 28th April and there were three more innovations in addition to the established agenda.

First, the BT Hot Air Balloon were invited to give spectators and keen photographers the opportunity to see and to photograph the racing from a different perspective (abandoned because of bad weather). Our own County Regiment, The Cheshires, were invited to put on a display and finally we introduced a new series called Formula Replica. However, following the dispute with the main club the previous year, the members of Area 15 of the Jaguar Drivers' Club had voted unanimously to form a new race organising club, the Cheshire Cats Car Club. This Meeting was therefore arranged by JDC Area 15 as their annual Area Day and the racing organised by the Cheshire Cats Car Club.

The Peter J Lambert Trophy donated by Club Secretary Penny Forsyth in memory of her father for fastest Jaguar saloon, Oulton Park 1982

Production Sports Car race, Snetterton, 1983.
Tim Sisson (Series 11 E-Type). Photographer Fred Scatley

Woodcote Corner at Silverstone, a traffic jam of Intermarque cars, 1983. Photographer Fred Scatley

Production Sports Car race, Silverstone.
John Simms presses hard on Ron Lea

Production Class Series III E-Type entering
Old Hall Corner, Oulton Park

The 3rd Cheshire Cats' Trophy Meeting

100 mile TROPHY Race,
CHAPMAN SPOONER Inter-Marque Challenge Championship Race.
Full supporting programme, Classic Saloons, Modified & Historic sports cars, M.G. etc.
1st race of new FORMULA REPLICA class.

BRITISH & EUROPEAN CHAMPION TRACTOR PULLERS

Tethered Hot Air Balloon rides – Magnificent view of the circuit!

OULTON PARK RACE CIRCUIT

Saturday 28th April 1984

Official Programme 50p

JAGUAR DRIVERS' CLUB – AREA 15

JAGUAR DRIVERS' CLUB
Area 15 Cheshire

INTRODUCTION

Following the established policy of the CHESHIRE CATS to make this annual Meeting an event which all the family can enjoy, not just the racing enthusiast, we have introduced another innovation this year and welcome the BRITISH TELECOM hot air balloon, which is sure to be in demand particularly by keen photographers wishing to have an original shot of this famous Northern race circuit. Hopefully Oulton Park is on its way to regaining its former glory with the extension to Island bend, incorporating two fast sections which should make our kind of car more competitive on the twisting parkland course.

The 100 miles TROPHY race for roadgoing sports cars has become a 'must' for the keen amateur driver and this year has been oversubscribed to such a degree that it may be necessary to arrange qualifying heats for the final in the future to avoid disappointment to competitors from all over the Country. A varied racing programme has been included to satisfy the interests of all Club racing enthusiasts from Classic Saloons to modern supersports cars, Historic sportscars to the new FORMULA REPLICA introduced for the first time by the CHESHIRE CATS' CAR CLUB. A cross-section of all that's best in the unique British Club racing scene.

Unfortunately plans for a Championship Tractor Pulling Contest fell through at the last moment; but we are pleased to welcome four of the most outstanding Tractors and competitors in Championship Pulling to-day, two of them with multiple Jaguar V.12 engines.

Following the tradition of J.D.C. Area days, a Concours d'Elegance will take place with Trophies for Best Jaguar Sports Car, Best Jaguar Saloon, Best Mark I/II Saloon and the ultimate Award for the All Comers' Trophy. If you think your car stands a chance entry forms are available at the Area 15 caravan.

All owners of Historic and interesting Jaguars can also take part in the CAVALCADE of JAGUARS at approximately 3.30 p.m. by contacting the Event Organisers in the Area 15 Caravan at the Register Compounds.

Welcome to our own County Regiment, the CHESHIRES, the recruiting Sergeant stands ready to offer the "Queen's Shilling" to any likely lad or lass. We hope you all have an enjoyable and memorable day with the CHESHIRE CATS.

Organising Committee

Chairman: R. V. Lea. **Race Organiser:** T. H. Rowe. **Events Organisers:** Mr. & Mrs. E. Farrall. **Concours Organiser:** D. J. Hough. **Committee Secretary:** S. D. Lea.

Acknowledgements

The Cheshire Cats' Car Club and the Jaguar Drivers' Club, Area 15, wish to thank the following for their kind and valuable help:
Members of the Clubs who have given their services as Honorary Officials and Marshals:
Chief Medical Officer and Colleagues;
The British Red Cross Society;
The Cheshire County Fire Brigade;
The Cheshire County Police;
Cheshire Car Circuit Ltd.

5

Oulton Park programme

Prior to this meeting I had contacted Eddie Shah, the newspaper mogul, who had thwarted the print unions, and he put me in touch with his security people. I managed to persuade John Webb of Cheshire Car Circuits Ltd, the owners of Oulton Park, to let us arrange our own circuit officials at much reduced cost. Eddie and his wife joined my wife and me in our Bucaneer caravan for lunch.

For this meeting I had persuaded Jim Marland of Proteus Cars to loan me one of his Jaguar C-Type replicas which I entered in the Modified and Formula Replica Race. Unfortunately, I had to retire in the race as the engine lost oil pressure. The V12 E-Type in the Intermarque was third in class. I was hoping to do well in the Cheshire Cats Trophy Race which had been reduced to 43 laps as I thought it was about time a Jaguar won it at last. Unfortunately, at Old Hall corner on the first lap I was pushed off the track by a Lotus 7 and lost a lot of time. He was behind me on the grid and yet was to finish third. I could not catch up and finished 8th. However, neither of us would have finished if we had collided and I saw him coming up the inside and avoided a coming-together which left me in the sand trap. Peripheral eyesight is very important in motor racing and I always had it checked at the start of each racing season. Jeremy Coulter, the driver of the Lotus 7, apologised after the race for his indiscretion.

Brands Hatch is a long way from Cheshire but I intended to support the Intermarque as captain of the team and travelled the 300-mile round trip to take part in this one race in which I finished well down in the pouring rain. Not my favourite circuit.

Finally in this limited season I competed in two Intermarque races, at Silverstone in July and Donington in August when I was fourth and fifth, respectively.

The Jaguar team win the Four Hour Relay at Oulton Park, 1983. Drivers left to right: Ron Lea, Don Shead, Malcolm Hamilton, pit manager Dave Nursey, driver Kirk Rylands. Photographer Peter Crummack

Tractor pulling contest at Oulton Park, 1984

Early days, Ron with some of his awards

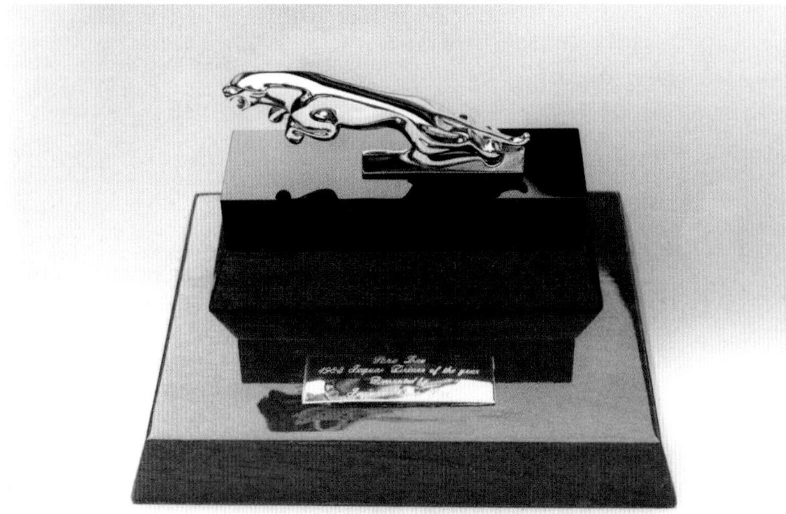

Jaguar Driver of the Year, 1983

Ron Lea receiving the Trophy from John Egan (Sir), CEO Jaguar Cars Ltd

Stephen Langton

FOLLOWING an accident during the Historic GP car race at Brands Hatch last Saturday, it is our sad duty to report the death of long time competitor Stephen Langton, aged 46.

He had been thrown from his car after it struck the Paddock Bend tyre wall and was lying on the grass verge when a following car struck him. He suffered serious multiple injuries and, despite the immediate attention of medical crews, both at the track and in hospital, he died at Queen Mary's Hospital in Sidcup.

Langton, from Hookwood in Surrey, had been a competitor in various forms of Historic racing for over 20 years and was renowned as an arch enthusiast. He will be remembered by fellow competitors as one of the mainstays of the sport with his B-Type Connaught, in which he was competing on Saturday, and a Lister Jaguar. He was one who thoroughly enjoyed his racing as a very competitive and brave driver. The Historic world has lost one of the leading lights in the sport and, to his wife Charlotte, and their four children, plus all family and friends, *Motoring News* extends its deepest sympathies.

Motoring News *announcement of the death of Steve Langton. (Correction, his wife's name is Elizabeth.) Receiving the Top Scorer in the Jaguar Intermarque team*

Stephen Langton's steering wheel kindly presented by Elizabeth Langton for the Top Scorer in the Jaguar Intermarque team. Received by Ron Lea on behalf of Chris Shipton

It was in the early 1980s that I became competition chairman of the JDC after Simon Watney and later a director of the club and vice chairman when John Owen was chairman. I was prepared to serve in this capacity because I believed if Jaguar were ever going to win the Intermarque Championship the board must subsidise the drivers by paying the entry fee. There was very little sponsorship in those days and amateur club racers did not look upon team events too kindly so that the best drivers were not interested. One of the most loyal competitors and a front runner and the highest scorer for the team at the time with his full point Lister Jaguar was Stephen Langton who was so tragically killed at Brands Hatch at the age of forty-six years. I was pleased to put his name forward for the Jaguar Driver of the Year Award which was awarded to him posthumously. Later his wife, Elizabeth, was to provide his Lister Jaguar steering wheel as the championship award for the top scorer Jaguar driver in the Intermarque.

It was in March 1998 that I wrote to Howard R. Davies, the General Manager of the Jaguar Daimler Heritage Trust, regarding the possibility of reintroducing the Jaguar Driver of the Year Award. Andrew Whyte had founded it and administered it annually since 1974 but it finished on his death. On 9th April 1998, I called at the Trust in Browns Lane, Coventry and discussed the proposition. He promised to look into it but nothing further was heard from him.

I was still interested in racing a more competitive car which could win races overall and not just class places and there were several efforts to achieve this which came to nought. Ron Beaty and I went down to Southampton to view an XJ13 replica at the invitation of Paul Hardy who was a JDC member and raced an XJ6. It was very strongly built but nothing further was heard from him and I assumed he had run out of money.

The other interesting project had been started by Brian Wilkinson who with friends in the GRP business had produced a replica of Bob Tullius' Group 44 E-Type. Don Law, who was working for me at the time, and I went down to see it in Suffolk. It would have utilised the Jaguar V12 engine and there was even a suggestion of a fibreglass monocoque (before carbon fibre) but I could not visualise it succeeding because of the lack of finance. Prior to this visit, I had been impressed with the success of Bob Tullius in his Group 44 Series III E-Type Jaguar in the USA and believed a replica of same would be successful in Europe. I therefore wrote to Bob to advise him of our plans and received an immediate reply stating it would be an honour to Group 44 if a replicar were manufactured in the UK and promising to support same with advice on specification, &c. I was to meet up with him at Le Mans when Group 44 entered their new mid-engined V12 Jaguar XJR5B.

The greatest potential race winner would have been a project involving Martin Robey and myself which was for a space frame chassis clad with Martin's E-Type panels in aluminium with a six-cylinder XK engine. Martin and myself visited Richard Owen at Silverstone, the successful designer of the Sports 2000 racing cars who had a considerable input into the design of the Jaguar XJ 220. Martin was not particularly impressed and suggested that he could build a space frame chassis with square section chrome molybdenum tube. He produced this but unfortunately the project was not developed, mainly because I realised that the chassis he had produced should have been for a large capacity Jaguar V12 engine and not the XK six-cylinder engine, a car which was eventually developed for Malcolm Hamilton by Rob Beere. Our car would have been much lighter with its space frame chassis and therefore a greater performance. I had regular correspondence with Lou Fidanza and his Gran Turismo Jaguar company when I was writing 'Competition News' and he sent me tapes of the races Freddy Baker, the 'Geordie Yank' his driver had been involved in when he had defeated the works support Datsun sports cars, particularly one driven by Paul Newman the famous film star, and I loaned these tapes to several Jaguar enthusiasts both here and abroad. He also sent me two sample Carillo piston rods, very light and strong which enabled him to regularly obtain 8000 rpm from his production 4.2-litre XK engine which were paramount in Freddy beating the modern

Replicar of Jaguar XJ13 racing car

Substantial chassis of Jaguar XJ Replicar with V12 engine

The very successful Group 44 Jaguar E-Type V12 roadster in American classic car races, Driver Bob Tullius

GRP body for replicar of Group 44 racing roadster

Japanese sports cars and even the large capacity American V8 Corvettes and Camaros. I was to meet both Lou and Freddy when they came over to England on a short visit. Freddy was to be presented with the Jaguar Driver of the Year award for his exploits.

1985 was another busy year and the photograph on page 109 shows a typical grid at the start of an Intermarque Race at Oulton Park showing Porsche, Aston Martin, AC Cobra, Jaguar (myself in the 4) and unusually an XJ6 (Laurence Sayers-Gillan). The photograph on page 101 of two E-Types dicing in Woodcote Corner at Silverstone is myself leading John Simms, the photograph on page 109 is at Mallory Park when I had a close dice with David Neil, also in an XK 6-cylinder engined E-Type.

The following season started as usual with a JDC meeting in March when I was third overall in the Production Car race in spite of the first signs of a major engine problem when the oil pressure was far too high but it was thought that it had something to do with the new high pressure gauge, and then at Silverstone in early April when the power was coming in surges and it would not go above 5000 rpm. Later that month the engine blew up in a big way on the fourth lap at Oulton Park when a connecting rod came through the side of the block. I was able to buy a new V12 engine from the Henleys when it was taken to Ron Beaty's who race prepared it and increased the bore to give 5.7-litre (5.3-litre standard) and fitted with Cosworth pistons and special camshaft.

Don Law had been helping me with race preparation on a part time basis and he was now to become employed full time by my company as garage manager and was keen to modify the car to make it more competitive. I agreed it was time this was done although wishing to retain it as a road going touring car. It was therefore taken to Moorland Classic Cars to have the rear wings 'teased out' to accommodate the new ten-inch minilite

Movie star Paul Newman (Datsun 280Z) congratulates Freddy Baker (E-Type) on winning the championship. Photographer Rus Snelbaker

wheels fitted with 23/59 TB 15 Michelin tyres. Although the new Jaguar engine had more power it was largely the 'footprint' of the tyres which gave the car increased performance with reduced lap times. I competed in twelve races this year, five of them Intermarque and at Mallory Park was the overall winner of the Jaguar Production Car race by some distance on a wet track.

The photograph on page 111 shows the semi-modified E-Type at Oulton Park but at the Donington Park meeting in August its engine was converted from four 2-inch SU carburettors to 45 DCOE Weber carburettors but they were not found to have any particular advantage. The photograph on page 113 shows the winning team in the Intermarque for 1986 with the drivers from the left:

Martin Wheatley (yellow E-Type), Chris Shipton (purple E-Type) Malcolm Hamilton (white E-Type), Ron Lea (red E-Type) and Dave Moore (red E-Type with silver nose). All the cars had six-cylinder XK engines except my V12, and Martin's car was fully modified in Class C. Chris's mildly modified in Class B and Malcolm's and Dave's fully modified in Class C. All were on slick tyres except the V12 on treaded tyres which was in Production Class A. The other high scorer was not present at the final Oulton Park round was Mike Tye with his Production Class A car series II E-Type with treaded tyres. The JDC team top scorer was Malcolm

Lou Fidanza's Gran Turismo Jaguar E-Type roadster, driver Freddy Baker

Hamilton, being presented with the award by myself. 1987 was to be the last season of Circuit Racing for this fifteen-year-old V12 car which commenced in March at Silverstone when I was fourth in class. The photograph on page 110 shows the dice between Richard Gordon (Porsche 911 Carrera) and myself at Copse Corner when I passed him on the inside to win by 7.1 seconds. My car is running on standard wheels with Yokohama tyres, not the wider wheels.

I was kindly invited to take part in the Classic Parade before the British Grand Prix in 1987 by the Secretary of the BRDC, the late Pierre Aumonier. We were supposed to do three laps and come in

Close dice between David Neill and Ron Lea at Mallory Park

Intermarque race at Oulton Park with conglomeration of different makes and models on the starting grid

when the chequered flag appeared. We were enjoying ourselves so much in front of an audience of many thousands that we carried on for a further three laps. At the end of this my car suffered an electrical 'glitch' and stopped. We were rescued by the race marshals and ignominiously towed in. Most embarrassing and I wrote to Pierre Aumonier later to apologise for delaying the start of the British Grand Prix which was famously won by Nigel Mansell from Nelson Piquet. Both my sons, Tony and Tim, joined me in this parade and the latter took the photographs through the windscreen.

Ron Lea (E-Type) overtakes Porsche 911 Carrera (R. Gordon) at Copse, Silverstone to cross the line 7.1 seconds ahead. Intermarque. Photographer Alan Hewitt

Ron Lea in semi-modified E-Type entering Old Hall Corner at Oulton Park. Contrast this with the earlier standard car at this corner

The photograph (right) at Mallory Park shows Malcolm Hamilton (modified E-Type), Ian Exeter (BLE modified XJS), and myself (semi-modified E-Type) on the outside at the start of the Jaguar Modified and Production race. The next photograph (right) is immediately after the start which is as far as my car was to travel as the differential broke and I was out of both races that day. Finally in October at Oulton Park I was fifth in class in the Intermarque and was first in class in the Modified/Historic race setting a record lap in the process. In the Intermarque Championship for 1987 the JDC team were second to the Porsche team and the final placings are listed herewith:

1987 Mallory Park, the front row of the modified Jaguar race with Malcolm Hamilton (modified E-Type) on pole with Ian Exeter (modified XJS) and Ron Lea (semi-modified E-Type)

Ron Lea makes the best start but immediately stops when the differential breaks

JDC INDIVIDUAL SCORES	
Ron Lea (full points)	72 pts.
Malcolm Hamilton – E-Type (half points)	71 ½ pts.
Mike Tye – E-Type (full points)	67 pts.
David Botting – XJ6 (three quarter points)	47 ¼ pts.
Laurence Sayers-Gillan – XJ 12 (half points)	15 pts.
Chris Shipton – E-Type (three quarter points)	12 pts.
Roger Bowman – XJS (half points)	8 ½ pts.
Mike Whitaker – E-Type (half points)	8 pts.
Ian Exeter – XJS (full points)	6 pts.
Martin Wheatley – E-Type (three quarter points)	3 pts.
TOTAL POINTS:	**325 ¾ pts.**

Mallory Park 2007 - Ron Lea stands between his 1972 Series III E-Type and his 2006 XK coupe before the 'back-to-back' comparison test. Ron in the standard production 4.2 litre XK and Paul Alcock in the race prepared 5.7 litre E-Type.

Moorland Classic Cars 'tease-out' the wings of the E-Type for wider wheels

My wife has supported me both in my business and in my motorsport hobby. In 1967 she was a shareholder and secretary in the new company Ronald V Lea Ltd and when I commenced club motor racing in 1977 we would travel to the circuit venues in a motor caravan where she would look after not only myself but quite often JDC team drivers and supporters in the championship. It is appropriate to gratefully acknowledge this assistance on the retirement from circuit racing of my Series III E-Type 2 + 2 coupe (5.7-litre V12) which she always called my 'mistress'.

During this ten-year period when I was involved in JDC administration as the chairman of the competition committee, chairman of the Cheshire Cats organising committee and vice chairman of the board of directors, etc, etc, she dealt with all my correspondence.

Ron Beaty adjusts the Weber carburettors before Donnington race

Team Captain Ron Lea presents Malcolm Hamilton with the Top Scorer cup after the mainly E-Type team won the 1986 Intermarque Championship. (Not present Mike Tye with PEE22 E-Type). Photographer Alan Hewitt

1987 British Grand Prix at Silverstone. Classic parade shown the chequered flag, but we did not stop!
Photographer Tim Lea

1987 British Grand Prix. Tim has an excellent view of the finish

Winner Nigel Mansell receives the plaudits of the crowd

Some of the trophies won by Ron Lea and the Jaguar Team

CHAPTER 15

My 'Mistress' Had To Go

It was a fitting end for this race prepared E-Type when it was the top scorer in the JDC Intermarque team in 1987, although the team were second to the Porsche Owners Club. During its mainly circuit racing career this basically standard production sports car over ten years completed in ninety-five circuit races as well as innumerable sprints and hill climbs and very demanding relays. It was never really suitable for club circuit racing because it was too heavy and had difficult handling which is why very few were raced by amateur club drivers. During its thirty-four years in my ownership it gave a lot of pleasure to myself as well as enjoyment to my wife and myself covering thousands of miles on continental tours. During this fiftieth anniversary year of the launch of the E-Type it will surely be seen with its present owner at celebration events. Before the car was sold in 2007 there was an opportunity to compare its performance with a new Jaguar XK coupe, 4.2-litre naturally aspirated, which I bought in September 2006 with my friend Paul Alcock, we were able to do this during the luncheon interval at the JEC track day at Mallory Park when although the track was damp this race prepared car now with automatic gearbox was nearly competitive with the more than thirty years of technical advanced engineering represented by the XK and there would have been little between them when the E-Type had its racing manual gearbox. However the superior comfort and handling of the XK was apparent even on a smooth race track which would have been accentuated

Race prepared semi-modified E-Type cockpit in touring guise

Ron Lea with his Series III E-Type Jaguar at the entrance to the JDC Area 18 meeting place. Not quite as fast as the English Electric Lightning behind!!

on the road. With my deteriorating physical condition this was the deciding factor in my decision to sell this well loved car.

Following my stroke in 1996 modifications were made to this Series III E-Type 2 + 2 coupe and the photograph shows the cockpit with its earlier automatic gearbox (later to have a five speed ZF) the air conditioning unit very necessary for continental tours, the sloping instrument panel and the original racing steering wheel taken from my first modified E-Type roadster which was crashed at Croft. The rear axle was replaced with a 2.88:1 differential which made it very quick on the open road.

At the third Cheshire Cats Trophy meeting at Oulton Park in 1984, as chairman of the organising committee I had introduced a new Racing Formula, Formula Replica. I had raced a Proteus Replica Jaguar C-Type in this race but did not finish. However there were two significant developments on this first race in this new Formula, one which was immediately apparent that on twisty club circuits the heavier replicas of the Jaguar C-Type and D-Type and Cobra, etc. would not be able to compete with the much lighter and smaller capacity Caterham 7 type of car. It would have been quite different if the races took place on Grand Prix circuits where the larger cars could have 'stretched their legs'.

The other problem was with regard to the rollover bars and for this first race we received a special dispensation from the RAC MSA that no rollover bars would be required on the replicas. It was in fact much later in 1988 when the championship started for this type of car that the RAC insisted that all entrants cars should have rollover bars. The original cars, i.e. C-Types, D-Types, Cobra, etc still do not have this safety requirement but on balance I considered it as a regulation that was worthwhile. However it had the effect of discouraging owners of the more expensive aluminium replicas who withdrew their support for the championship series even though detachable roll over bars could have been fitted. This short-sighted decision was understandable but disappointing as the maximum number of entrants was essential to get the Championship off the ground. It was in the January 1988 issue of the *Jaguar Driver* magazine under my article 'Wide Angle' that this new racing formula was introduced to club racing.

THE SPIRIT OF JAGUAR

Ron's D-Type replicar in Ecurie Ecosse colours at speed, from an original painting by Scott Bevis

I was undecided whether to enter an L. R. Roadster D-Type replica myself or a Challenger E-Type replica. I had visited the Challenger factory in Cornwall and met Frank Costin who had been contracted by Derek Robinson to engineer the latest version with a Jaguar engine instead of the Rover V8 engine and its suspension. I stayed overnight in a local hotel where Frank was staying and it was in the early hours of the next day that we eventually stopped talking about motor racing, particularly Le Mans and the disastrous Maserati 4.5-litre coupe he designed for Stirling Moss in 1957, for which the body builders Zagato did not follow his instructions, so that it was a complete disaster. He was more famous for his design of the aerodynamic body of the World Championship winning Vanwall Grand Prix car.

After racing an E-Type for so many years I was interested in continuing with the association and eventually after Challenger had moved to a new factory in Corby, Northants, they offered to part-sponsor the lightweight E-Type replica for the Paladin Shield Historic Replicar Championship but unfortunately I was committed to racing the L. R. Roadster D-Type replica.

There had been much increased interest from potential competitors for the new championship following publicity in the national motor press during January and it was now necessary to form a registration committee of experienced race engineers and competitors as follows:

Brian Wilkinson (race engineer & specialist on safety systems)
John Pearson (historic Jaguar competitor and race engineer)
John Atkins (historic Cobra competitor & specialist)
Bryan Wingfield (race engineer & GT 40 specialist)
myself as chairman

The Paladin Shield Historic Replicar Championship, 1988. Registration and test day at Silverstone. Ron Lea's LR Roadster replicar D-Type ready for inspection. In background Left to Right: Ron Lea, Brian Wilkinson, Gordon Viola (MSA technical inspection) in front of Fiat Ducato motor caravan used by Ron and Sheila to tow the race car and support the series drivers

The first registration day was scheduled for the 30th March at Silverstone when potential competitors had to present their cars for inspection. The intention was to create a championship for amateur drivers in two-seater sports cars of similar eras without allowing the later models with more modern technology to dominate the opposition. For example the Jaguar C-Type and D-Type of the mid-1950s would be competing against the AC Cobra and GT 40 of the mid-1960s. One well known Jaguar racing engineer advised that he considered the single streamlined aero screen on the Cobra to be worth 100 bhp in engine power compared to a full-width/high-windscreen. This was not popular with Cobra replica drivers because of restricted visibility in bad conditions. But it was pointed out to them that they already had a considerable engine capacity advantage. This also applied to the GT40 replica which utilised the 5.7-litre Ford V8 but their advantage of a mid-engine configuration was one which could not be penalised and resulted in due course in controversy when experienced drivers threatened to run away with races.

A C-Type replicar with owner Nigel Forsyth sitting in car ready for inspection with competitor Ron Lea and Tim Sisson talking to Colin McMeekin the MD of sponsors Paladin Jaguar.

The detailed regulations were set-out in my series of 'Wide Angle' articles during 1986 in the *Jaguar Driver* magazine including the unfortunate 'break-away' by some of the competition committee of the Jaguar Driver's Club led by Mr T. H. Rowe which was an unnecessary problem at this time and is detailed in the 1988 March issue of the club magazine the *Jaguar Driver*.

In fact it was because of a request from the late Andrew Whyte, PR and historian of Jaguar Cars to get together old acquaintances and friends to attend the Cheshire Cats at the Oulton Park race meeting that I collected Jack Broadhead, the 1950s entrant/sponsor of a D-Type driven by Bob Berry, from his home in Cheshire in my Jaguar XJ6 Series 1 and took him to the race meeting. During

Peripheral eyesight is an advantage! A Porsche pushes Ron's car off coming into Druids Corner at Brands Hatch but saving any damage. The Canadian driver apologised after the race

the journey he asked me who was the clerk of the course. When I told him Tom Rowe, who had been employed by him as transport manager in the 1950s, he made a derogatory remark which I did not query at the time but made me realise loyalty to Tom Rowe would be misplaced in the future, and when the arrangements were being made for the following year's Cheshire Cats meeting I telephoned Peter Harrop (who was a qualified RAC MSA official as a clerk of the course who lived in Poynton in Cheshire and whose father had been a Jaguar enthusiast and competed in a Jaguar SS100) and asked him if he would act as clerk of the course at our next race meeting, but disappointingly he was committed on the April date concerned although he was very sorry he could not take up the offer. I have always believed if we had been able to replace Tom Rowe at this time his aspirations to start a competing Jaguar club would have been curbed, it seriously disrupted Jaguar amateur club racing and was the beginning of the end of Jaguar Area 15's register day and the Cheshire Cats Car Club meeting at Oulton Park. The resulting Jaguar Car Club which he founded, and which I was asked to be a member of but declined, will always be an embarrassment to those JDC officials who succumbed to his persuasion, as it folded within a few years.

I have since found out from an ex-chairman of the JCC that they have 'lost' the Cheshire Cats Trophy which was originally located by the JDC Area 15 secretary, Penny Forsyth, in a Chester jewellers shop and bought by Kevin Rigby's employers and gifted to the JDC Area 15. This prestigious trophy was never won by a Jaguar, but this loss is an example of the irresponsibility of those race and club officials and so-called members who were disloyal to their club.

The registration and test day at Silverstone was very successful with the potential of twenty-five historic replicas for the coming season. However, of the four arranged race dates the first one at Oulton Park on the 23rd April was cancelled owing to the 'shenanigans' of Mr Rowe and his cohorts which was particularly unfortunate to myself as it was my home circuit and was the venue of the first Cheshire Cats Trophy Meeting in 1982. The first race therefore was at Silverstone on the 21st May which Tim Sisson in the Works Cobra Replicar was to win from Roger Warrell in his Jaguar C-Type Replicar with myself and the LR Roadster D-Type third. All within six seconds of each other.

A close dice between Ron Lea (D-Type Replicar) and Roger Warrell (C-Type Replicar) at Silverstone.
Photographer Chris Harvey

Unfortunately at the second round at Donington Park on the 25th June only a total of six historic replicars were entered and the organisers, the British Motor Racing Marshals Club, quite naturally wished to have a full race entry and combined the oversubscribed kit car race with our Paladin championship round. This was not acceptable to our registration committee and our cars were withdrawn at the third round. Again at Donington Park on the 6th July the race was stopped after five laps when a specially invited Triumph TR7 was in a collision with Richard Tyzack in his Jaguar C-Type Replicar which blocked the track. Tim Sisson won again but this time I was second with Roger Warrell third.

At the fourth round at Mallory Park on the 31st July I had engine problems and did not finish and the race was won again by Tim Sisson and Roger Warrell second. Our concern over the advantage of the Cobra was being realised but it was being accentuated by being a Works entry with a very experienced driver. The fifth round at Castle Coombe on the 6th August resulted in a good win for Roger Warrell (Heritage C-Type Replicar) after my D-Type Replicar was taken off the front of the grid within two minutes of the start by an over-zealous official after a leak left oil the size of a fifty pence coin on the line as we waited for the start!

The 6th and final round was at Donington Park on the 23rd October and saw the entry for the first time of an original historic AC Cobra by Aidan Mills-Thomas with an Intermarque specification which helped it to win ahead of the championship leader Tim Sisson with the Works Cobra Replicar. I was fourth in the final round. The officials of the A.M.O.C. (Aston Martin Owners Club) who organised the Intermarque Challenge Championship would not allow Historic Replicars to compete in the Jaguar team which supported the series from its beginning and won same in 1986. A short-sighted decision as it now has little support overall.

I was very pleased that an original historic car had won the race because it would hopefully show other owners of these valuable cars that they had nothing to fear from the competition of these historic replicars. In fact I had previously asked Mr F. R. W. 'Lofty' England, who was instrumental in the Jaguar success at the Le Mans in the 1950s, his opinion of historic replicar racing and he was in total support and suggested that original historic models should be encouraged to enter.

Another well known historic car personality who was also supportive was Denis Jenkinson the famous journalist with *Motor Sport* magazine. He wrote to me in March 1988; a copy of his letter is reprinted on page 124. He showed an 'open-mindedness' lacking in other so-called 'purist' journalists and motor traders and entrants/competitors whilst he was undoubtedly the most experienced and clear thinking journalist of them all. Witness his incredible ability as the co-pilot of the Mercedes Benz 300 SLR in the Mille Miglia with Stirling Moss leaving Fangio the World Champion driving solo well behind in spite of the Argentinian's vast experience in South American road races.

Probably because of my widely acknowledged experience of motor racing as a spectator commencing in 1948 with the first British Grand Prix and sports racing cars from the early 1950s, Le Mans etc, I was able to propose and have accepted the regulations for the new historic replicars finely tuned by the committee. Basically my aspirations were for it to be a level playing field for Jaguar engine replicas but with the loss of the aluminium bodied Jaguar replicas because their owners were not prepared to fit a rollover bar, the championship eventually became open to all kinds of unsuitable kit cars which have in the twenty-first century proliferated to such an extent.

The inaugural season for this new championship had been relatively successful and Paladin Jaguar agreed to sponsor same again for 1989. Races were organised at Silverstone, Donington, Mallory, Spa Francorchamps, Mallory, Pembrey, Snetterton and Pembrey again. The event at Spa in Belgium was the first time these particular championship cars had competed abroad and it was very interesting for myself as I had visited the circuit as a spectator for the European Grand Prix in 1952. It was always looked upon as a very dangerous circuit because of its variable weather conditions over its extreme length and several British drivers had been killed there including Dick Seaman (Mercedes Benz) in 1939 and Archie Scott-Brown (Lister Jaguar) in 1958. Although the circuit was reduced in length from the original, John Gregson (LR Roadster D-Type Replicar) was to crash on the second lap. He hit the Armco barrier at one of the fastest corners just before the 'bus stop' corner when just in front of myself. He was to escape injury but as he had driven his car to the circuit from the UK it was so badly damaged it was not roadworthy.

Fortunately as I had trailered my car I was able to load his car onto my trailer and bring it back for him whilst my son Tim drove my car on the return journey. Roger Warrell (Heritage C-Type Replicar) was to win the Paladin section of the race with Nick Taylor (LR Roadster D-Type Replicar) second and myself (LR Roadster D-Type Replicar) third.

End of Season party. Ron Lea and Nick Taylor open-up the 'Really tried hard' Trophy prepared by Heritage Engineering's Roger Warrell and Jack Frost

At the end of the season a dinner dance and award ceremony was arranged at the Rothley Court Hotel in Leicestershire when the good spirit of the Championship throughout the season was demonstrated by the 'Really Tried Hard Trophy' which caused much hilarity. The Championship awards were presented as follows – Roger Warrell, first overall and Jaguar Class winner. Nick Taylor, second in Jaguar Class and myself third in Jaguar Class. Tim Sissons, first in Cobra Class, Paul Bevis second in Cobra Class and Cheng Lim third in Cobra Class.

For the third year in succession Paladin Jaguar agreed to sponsor the Championship and I announced in the April issue of the *Jaguar Driver* magazine that for the 1990 season.

Chris Robinson was taking over as Historic Replicar Liaison because I was finding it impossible to do the administration whilst taking part in

The wonderfully high spirited party with all the winners showing off their Trophies in an exuberant manner, Rothley Court Hotel, Leicestershire

two championship series, the Paladin and the Intermarque. I had decided at the end of the previous year that my business commitments must take priority in the short term so I took a sabbatical from racing in 1990 at least until the end of the year. I employed Chris at Arleigh for a short period to make sure he was competent, but he was to experience a lack of co-operation from the JDC secretary.

The 'level playing field' we had hoped to achieve amongst these three different makes of historic replicars (that is Jaguar SS100, C-Type and D-Type, Cobra and GT40) to give close and competitive racing was beginning to unravel when Trevor Taylor in his GT40 was to win three consecutive races still with the novices compulsory plate on the rear of his car. Although it was clear that Trevor Taylor had natural ability my original concern that this mid-engined later model would dominate every race especially if experienced drivers became involved was soon to prove correct. However in the short term new more powerful entrants appeared i.e. Roger Warrell, last year's Champion now in a 5.7-litre Heritage Lister-Chevrolet 'Nobbly' Replicar and Nick Taylor 3.8-litre Heritage Lister-Jaguar 'Nobbly' Replicar and Leslie 'Jack' Frost in a very quick SS100 Replicar.

It was at the Cheshire Cats Trophy Race (100 miles) in very wet conditions that Mike Wilds, a former BRM Grand Prix driver joined Trevor Taylor in his GT40 when the combination of extra traction from his mid-engined car together with a very experienced driver was to result in it lapping the entire field except for Nick Taylor (Heritage 'Nobbly'). There were a further four GT40 cars in the offing, one of which was to be driven by Ray Mallock, another professional driver.

Richard Tyzack (competitor) presents Sheila with a bouquet of flowers for her support to the drivers throughout the season

In my 'Wide Angle' article in November issue of the *Jaguar Driver* magazine I reviewed the then current situation and, in particular, the lack of eligibility control of the Paladin Shield Championship since I passed it over and I suggested certain amendments to the regulations including cross ply tyres either 'L'or 'M' sections and that the Cobra entrants should only be allowed eight-inch wide wheel rims, etc and I even went so far as to suggest that the Championship should be for pre-60s sports

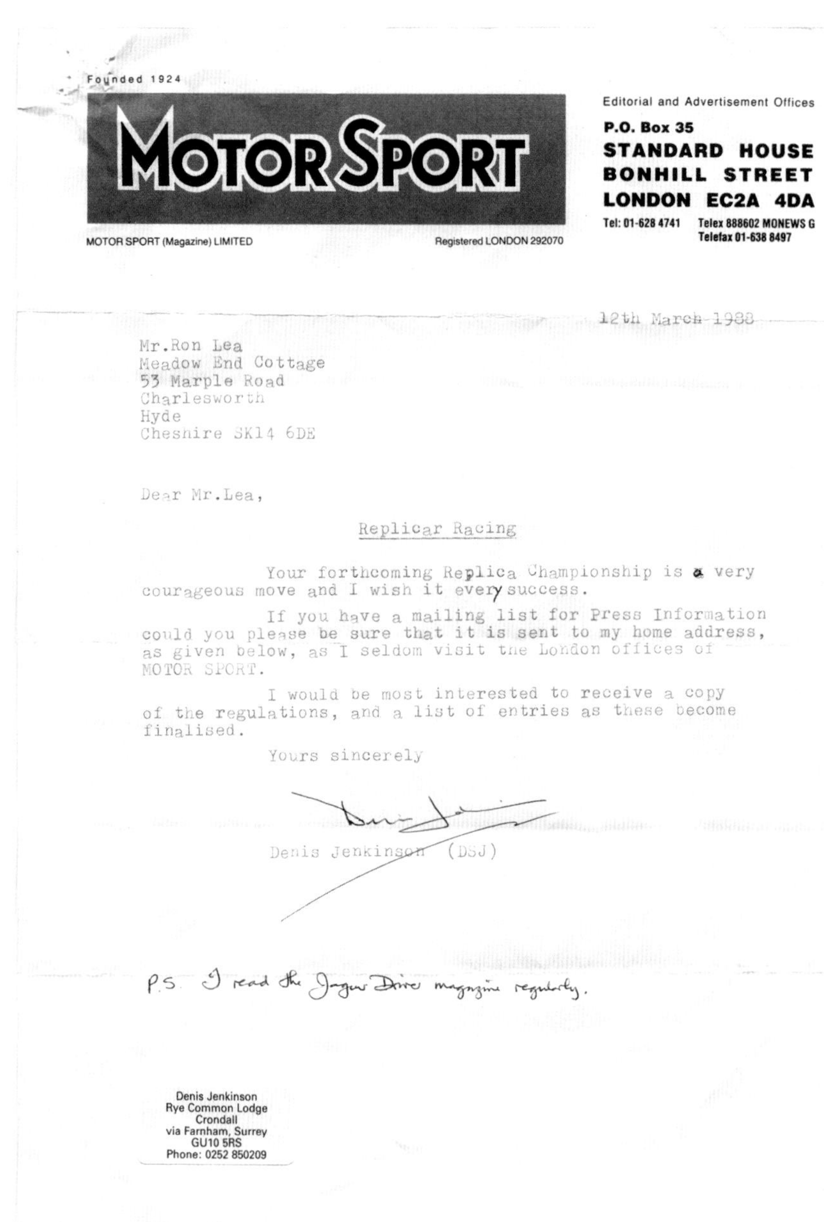

Founded 1924

MOTOR SPORT

Editorial and Advertisement Offices
P.O. Box 35
STANDARD HOUSE
BONHILL STREET
LONDON EC2A 4DA
Tel: 01-628 4741 Telex 888602 MONEWS G
Telefax 01-638 8497

MOTOR SPORT (Magazine) LIMITED Registered LONDON 292070

12th March 1988

Mr.Ron Lea
Meadow End Cottage
53 Marple Road
Charlesworth
Hyde
Cheshire SK14 6DE

Dear Mr.Lea,

Replicar Racing

Your forthcoming Replica Championship is a very courageous move and I wish it every success.

If you have a mailing list for Press Information could you please be sure that it is sent to my home address, as given below, as I seldom visit the London offices of MOTOR SPORT.

I would be most interested to receive a copy of the regulations, and a list of entries as these become finalised.

Yours sincerely

Denis Jenkinson (DSJ)

P.S. I read the Jaguar Driver magazine regularly.

Denis Jenkinson
Rye Common Lodge
Crondall
via Farnham, Surrey
GU10 5RS
Phone: 0252 850209

Letter from Denis Jenkinson, Motor Sport, *1988*

racing cars only which would eliminate both the Cobra and the GT40 and that we should campaign to have the Jaguar E-Type Replicar included.

Although these recommendations were somewhat 'over the top' to Cobra and GT40 drivers, it was a tactic to get these competitors to realise that unless there was a 'level playing field' the series would not survive.

However, these and other recommendations were not even discussed by some competitors who could not accept any of these suggestions and resulted in a 'break away' by some of the comparative new boys who were not members of the JDC and had no allegiance to same. Having relinquished my control of historic replicar racing the current chairman of the Jaguar Drivers' Club decided to give two of its motor racing championships to other clubs, i.e the Top Gear to the Historic Sports Car Club and the Historic Replicar to the British Racing Sports Car Club.

This decision was taken without reference to the founders of these championships and when one considers the JDC originated with motor racing as its principal activity it was an autocratic decision which spelled the end of JDC organised classic car racing which began in 1956 and allowed the new Jaguar Car Club and later the Jaguar Enthusiast Club free rein to promote their motor racing aspirations. The new replacement club secretary was so shocked at this decision that she telephoned me to advise of developments, although later denied such a communication took place no doubt because of repercussions to her employment position. Therefore the British Racing Sports Car Club organised the championship rounds and it was undeniable that they would be able to offer races at the famous circuits which the drivers understandably preferred.

However, with due respect to the BRSCC and I was a member for many years, I cannot see them allowing these series to develop along the lines originally envisaged. Inevitably due to commercial pressures the control

The Ron Lea Founder's Cup kindly provided by the co-ordinators of the SR and GT Challenge series, Cheng Lim and partner Jane, a continuation of the Paladin Shield format

Close-up of the inscription on the Ron Lea Founder's Cup

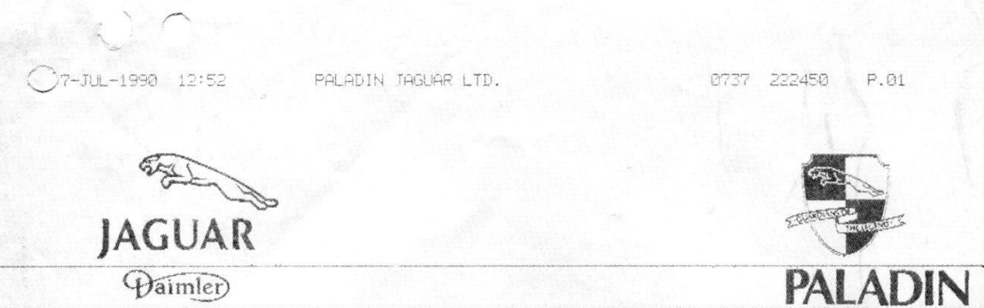

17-JUL-1990 12:52 PALADIN JAGUAR LTD. 0737 222450 P.01

JAGUAR

Daimler

PALADIN

33-35 Bell Street
Reigate
Surrey RH2 7AJ

Tel No: 0737 241100
Fax No: 0737 222450

TO: Mr R Lea

FAX NUMBER: 061 449 8683

FROM: C J T McMeekin

NUMBER OF PAGES: 1

DATE: 17 July 1990

MESSAGE:

Copy of a fax sent to The Board of Directors, Jaguar Drivers Club

Gentlemen,

<u>PALADIN SHIELD HISTORIC REPLICAR CHAMPIONSHIP</u>

I note with regret some of the recent correspondence circulating with regard to the above series. In particular I was sorry to see a letter from Mr Chris Robinson implying that Mr Ronald Lea was acting as a sponsors representative.

I am most anxious that this series is not sabotaged by personal ambitions or quasi - political considerations, so I would therefore be most grateful if you will give consideration to my following comments:-

1. My company's initial support for the series was discussed just prior to the unfortunate J.D.C/J.C.C schism. Whilst this situation did damage to media support for the series introduction it was Mr Lea's pragmatic and dedicated approach which retained and confirmed our sponsorship.

2. It has always been the situation that my personal confidence has been vested in Mr Lea and that I expect him to directly control sponsorship funds.

+3. Mr Lea is no way a sponsors representative, but as representative of the J.D.C he has my total trust and confidence.

I believe that there is considerable risk of the championship moving away from J.D.C control as a result of competitor's pressure and I would very much regret such a concurrence.

Please let us work together to ensure that this exciting and impressive facet of motorsport retains a Jaguar connection.

Yours sincerely

C J T McMeekin

Registered Office

of eligibility which is essential if the championship is to retain its aspirations will become even more of a 'grey' area and not only will the mid-engine car dominate but smaller lightweight kit cars would be entered. In fact this is what has happened. It is now dominated by many different models of kit cars and the GT40 had disappeared from historic replicar racing.

In due course the BRSCC relinquished the replica racing formula and it was taken over by the 750 Motor Club (ironically the founders of kit car racing) and it was renamed the SR & GT (Sports Racing & Gran Turismo) Challenge. On the 17th October 2010 I was asked by Cheng Lim and partner Jane co-ordinators of the series to present the Ron Lea Founders Trophy to the seasons winner with a Jaguar engine, the historic replicar D-Type of Tim Falce.

This surprising development confirmed my suspicion that some of the entrants and drivers in the Paladin Shield series were regretting the collapse of a championship for these replicars/replicas of famous sports racing cars of yesteryear and were disappointed at the increasing influx of lightweight kit cars which have such an advantage on slower club circuits because of their power to weight ratio and manoeuvrability.

Therefore I propose that historic replica motor racing should be reintroduced basically to the original Paladin Shield format and would be open to replicas of Jaguar SS100, classic Jaguar XK, C-Type, D-Type, E-Type with derivatives including Lister Jaguar, Lister Chevrolet, Kougar, Ronart, etc. Also A.C. Cobra and any other front-engined replicas of classic 2-seater sports cars which meet the regulations such as the Austin Healey, Triumph TR7. The new series could be co-ordinated by a new motor racing club HISTORIC ENCORE RACING CLUB. Encore meaning "once again", appropriate in this context.

No mid or rear engine race cars would be included and the engine capacity would generally exclude kit cars. A recommended minimum 3000cc engine capacity either naturally aspirated, supercharged or turbocharged and a maximum capacity of 5700cc naturally aspirated although this could be increased as long as there is a "level playing field" for all entrants to the enjoyment and support of the paying public. Interested parties should contact myself.

CHAPTER 16

Return to Classic Motorsport

In 1992 the famous ex-Warren Pearce fully modified E-Type racing car, Registration No. 310 WK was rebuilt after its crash at Aintree in 1982 by John Oxborough. He returned it to its original specification as a circuit racing car and it was fitted with a 4.4-litre XK engine with 48 DFA Dellorto carbs, four speed manual gearbox and the unique fabricated and fully rose jointed independent rear suspension, four pot Can Am front brakes and original racing exhaust. It has a Lenham hard top. Although it had been completed in a Circuit Racing specification it was intended to be used as a hill climb/sprint car only. However there was always the possibility that at the age of sixty-one years I may be tempted to start circuit racing again in due course. A hill climb specification would have involved smaller slick tyres which would 'heat up' on the slower hill climb corners and in fact at one event at Loton Park an Avon tyre technician checked the temperature of the tyres of competitors after a run up the hill and found that my extra wide tyres were still completely cold. This contrasted with other specialist hill climb car tyres which had reached a temperature that gave them better grip.

The collection area for the Jaguar Replicars at Prescott hill climb. Courtesy the International E-Type Register of the JDC

The fully modified racing E-Type restored by John Oxborough for circuit racing at the BARC Yorkshire Harewood hill climb venue. Photographer Tony Lea

The hill climbs at Loton Park were organised by the Hagley & District Light Car Club and its competition secretary, Dave Parr, was always most helpful in trying to arrange a Historic Replicar Class which unfortunately could not attract the entries. Several excellent times over the years with this fully modified Jaguar E-Type.

In spite of this disadvantage this modified E-Type was very competitive and was to achieve several class wins during the season at the BARC at Harewood and at Loton Park.

In fact the International E-Type Register committee had invited me to one of their meetings to ask how they could interest their Register members in the future instead of the normal static display on Register days. I suggested to them that it would be ideal if they could arrange with a hill climb venue to co-operate in this way and in due course they were able to arrange an E-Type Day with the Bugatti Owners Club at their Prescott Hill Climb, which has become a very popular event over the years.

In the meantime I was to be awarded the Hatfields of Sheffield Jaguar Trophy and the Guyson Sandblast Trophy for 1992 for hill climb successes.

A 'bit of spit and polish' will not make it go faster, but admired by spectators

The famous ex-Warren Pearce E-Type 310WK, the most competitive race car owned and raced by Ron Lea. Photographer Tony Lea

Just a hint of wheelspin at the off Harewood hill climb Photographer Tony Lea

A rather wide circuit race car for the narrow Harewood hill climb for Ron Lea's fully modified E-Type

CHAPTER 17

Historic Replicar Register

It was in November 1994 that I suggested that a new register should be formed to cater for these replicars of the famous jaguar models including the SS100, C-Type, D-Type, XJ13 and E-Type. The suggestion received support from members of the Jaguar Drivers' Club so I decided to proceed with the formation for this new register and I was pleased to have the help of Frank Whitby who was a retired chartered electronic engineer and had built his own Jaguar D-Type replicar with fuel injection from a Series III XJ.

In the 1995 January issue of the club magazine the origins and aims of the register were set out for discussion by members. In due course the formation for this new register was passed by a majority of members at the following AGM. During this period although it was quite successful I had decided to sell the modified E-Type Roadster 310WK and build a new historic replicar D-Type Jaguar with a supercharged engine.

When the Jaguar factory introduced the XJR supercharged saloon it reawakened an interest I always had in forced induction originating in my following of motorsport immediately postwar.

The latest historic replicar owned by the author but loaned to race drivers. Supercharged 4 litre Jaguar powered D-Type historic replicar in American colours entered under the name Encore Racing

It was then the accepted way of increasing the power and particularly the torque of racing engines. I had therefore decided a competitive Jaguar sports car in hill climbs would need to be much lighter and more compact and preferably have a supercharged engine giving lots of torque low down. The D-Type was the second racing sports car Jaguar Cars have ever made and consequently had the compact dimensions required, i.e. seven-foot six-inch wheelbase, four-foot four-inch track, with overall dimensions approximately thirteen feet long and five feet five inches wide (310WK is fourteen feet long and six feet one inch wide).

Through a special arrangement with the factory I was able to get hold of a 4-litre twenty-four-valve standard AJ16 engine with Eaton supercharger and intercooler together with the latest five-speed Getrag gearbox. The chassis is a standard D-Type replica which was designed for the XK power unit and would not accommodate the AJ16 engine mainly because of the extra width of the supercharger and intercooler and the fact that the engine leans over fifteen degrees. The chassis incorporated the fully rose jointed independent suspension front and rear, the latter based on the fabricated design fitted to 310WK and designed originally by Warren Pearce.

Ron Lea with his new car and its supercharged Jaguar engine and cockpit unique in race events in 1997

The author congratulates Adam Crowton on his first win at Snetterton

Ron Lea tries his hand in the new car, Prescott. International E-Type Register

Another essential feature as far as I was concerned was a close fitting racing seat so that I did not depend on the racing harness to hold me in position against the high g-forces. This had been a distinct disadvantage when I was racing the D-Type in the Paladin series. I now have a foam moulded GRP seat to my own shape. The only trouble is that since it was moulded I have been dieting so I might still be 'floating about like a pea in a pod'. The new car unusually has servo brake assistance and whilst there would be a loss of 'feel' the assistance is needed to facilitate late braking with a football-damaged knee and will be less tiring when the car is used for touring as originally expected.

Trevor Crisp, Chief Engineer at Jaguar, has been most helpful, as have his managers, particularly Ian Eddington. The engine performance figures of this completely standard engine with a catalyst exhaust system was 308.9 bhp at 5000 rpm, and more significantly for hill climbing 389 lbs of torque at 3000 rpm. The building and development of this car was delayed which eventually was completed by Eike Wellhausen at Chesterfield.

It was also at this time that I suggested a memorial should be created to Mike Hawthorn, the first British World Champion in 1958, and more significantly the E-Type Register very kindly invited the Historic Replicar Register to their E-Type Day at Prescott Hill in June where members were able to take their road-going replicas up this speed hill climb.

However it was in July 1996 that I had a stroke whilst attending a meeting at the Tickled Trout Hotel at Preston, Lancashire, and I was taken to the Preston Royal Infirmary. Although initially it was thought to be a mild stroke, it was in fact much more severe and because I had private insurance I was collected by ambulance and taken to the Alexandra Hospital in Cheadle, Cheshire, where I remained for nearly three months. It left me hemiplegic on the right hand side without the use of my right hand and arm and through 'wear and tear' in the last fifteen years I have gradually deteriorated physically but thankfully not mentally.

First race for friend Paul Alcock at Snetterton, April, 2011

HISTORIC REPLICAR COMMITTEE

Ron Lea outlines the Origins and Aims

ACKNOWLEDGEMENT – Beginning with the John Egan era at Jaguar Cars Limited, the Factory have had a benign attitude towards reproductions of their famous obsolete models and the new management deserve the sincere thanks of all Jaguar enthusiasts and Historic Replicar manufacturers for continuing with this policy for what would almost certainly be looked upon in Law as copyright infringement. All publicity is good publicity it has been said, and the fact that Jaguar components and engines, albeit usually second hand, are used in the building of these copies, must have a bearing on their attitude, which is why the Historic Committee must ensure that a high standard is maintained.

DEFINITION –The word Replica is often incorrectly used to describe these reproductions. It is quite clearly defined in the Oxford dictionary as the work of the original artist and therefore in this context can only accurately be used to describe a car made by the original manufacturer, i.e. Jaguar Cars. The word Replicar is a combination of words and not listed in any dictionary; however it is a thoroughly modern term to describe a car which has only appeared in the last 20 years, and is a copy of the original Works car, having an exact profile but varying slightly in dimensions. It should not have the badges of the original car and the Committee will discourage the use of same. The word Historic is appropriate because the original cars are obsolete, and were produced at a time generally looked upon as the Historic period in motoring circles.

SPECIFICATION – Since the original models were designed and manufactured, vehicle technology and materials have developed substantially. GRP (Fibreglass) has enabled an accurate profile to be achieved, in spite of complex curves at low cost; whilst the skills of the original panel beaters have survived so that accurate aluminium bodies are available today, albeit at much higher cost. Mass produced Jaguar components including the engine are available second hand, which if in good condition or overhauled, give an inbuilt safety margin and longevity. The "donor" car components were designed by experts for saloon cars weighing at least twice as much as the new Replicar. The ubiquitous XK engine in various capacities, is generally the choice of the Replicar builder; but the Committee wishes to encourage the use of later Jaguar engines now that they are becoming available at very reasonable prices. The AJ6 model is a very advanced engine with 24 valves and some 2cwt lighter than the XK model. In addition they are often available with 5 speed Gertrag manual boxes, which makes a very tempting package in a lightweight, good handling Historic Replicar. Could be turbocharged or supercharged for even greater performance! The advent of special induction systems to allow carburettor installation will assist the amateur builder in making his decision to install this up to date power transmission. Those that believe that the use of this newer engine would be inappropriate in a Historic Replicar, should consider the similar "evolution" of the Historic Replicar SS100, the original car had the OHV engine supplied by the Standard Motor Co. in 2½ and 3½ litre capacities; whereas these excellent reproductions use the XK engine, with considerable advantage. Equally important other components have advanced and modern suspensions can be utilized to keep the Historic Replicar if not abreast, at least in contact with latest developments, particularly if changes are made to the Construction and Use regulations for road use.

PURPOSE – The Committee will bring together Historic Replicar owners by means of a common interest in social events, concours, rallies, technical topics, Factory visits, competition, etc., and whilst the basic parameters will be strictly adhered to, will be devoted to the aim of widening the interest and knowledge in the construction, driving, maintenance and improvement of Jaguar based Historic Replicars.

24 VALVE AJ6 ENGINE WOULD BE ADVANTAGEOUS – IF YOU COULD FIT IT IN!

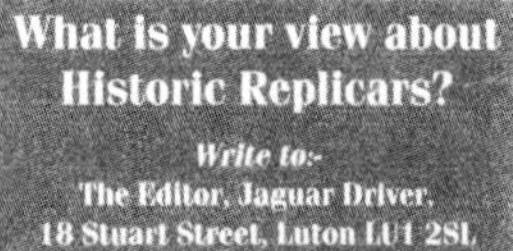

COMMITTEE MEMBER FRANK WHITBY'S D TYPE REPLICAR HAS FUEL INJECTION.

10

Jaguar Driver, January 1995

Initially therefore the car was loaned to Adam Crowton who was a foreman at a Jaguar main dealer and later worked at the Jaguar Experimental Depot at Gaydon in Warwickshire. Later it was loaned to Nick Taylor who I had raced against in the Paladin Series with a similar D-Type replicar and by 2002 although my disability prevented the use of the manual gearbox I had the car fitted with a 'Duck' clutch which has the appearance of a duck's beak and fits on the gear change lever and so is hand controlled. After an appointment at the RAC MSA for an interview I was granted a limited hill climb/sprint licence and attempted a comeback to motorsport at Loton Park Hill Climb. With the assistance of my oldest son, Tony, I was able to complete the practice and the two official hill climbs but the times were not competitive. As I was over 70 years old at the time and my mobility was severely restricted I decided to call it a day as far as competitive motorsport was concerned. Before practice started at Loton Park I met Sir Michael Leighton, the owner of the parkland, whilst on my battery powered buggy, and he suggested I should do a climb on this buggy. With a top speed of 8 mph it would hardly be spectacular! However I did the climb along the parallel pedestrian foot path and still managed to do a somersault on the way down.

Since then the Racing D-Type has been loaned to two other drivers but currently is being loaned to my good friend Paul Alcock who has not raced previously and is in his first season. Paul was to become a committee member for the England/Hawthorn Memorial Appeal and was the donor of the third prize. More of this later.

Following the launch of the Historic Replicar Register at the AGM of the Jaguar Drivers' Club in October 1995 with a vote of ninety-three for and thirty-six against, the secretary/correspondent Frank Whitby began to write monthly articles on the progress of the Register whilst I continued to include sometimes contentious comments under the heading of 'Wide Angle'. This latter heading had been created by John Foster, a long-time member who belonged to the family who founded and still owned the Black Dyke Mills in Yorkshire, famous for its brass band. 'Wide Angle' was presenting views and arguments on Jaguar matters with the engineering description of the Jaguar XK engine head casting of this very famous engine. John Foster agreed to sponsor a Jaguar club racing team through his company, the Black Dyke Jaguar Team for the Intermarque Challenge Championship and the Sir William Lyons Relay Team but which collapsed through the incompetence of the JDC head office at the time. Fortunately these two prestigious championships were won in due course in 1986 and 1983, respectively.

Over the next few years the HRR (Historic Replicar Register) was to have more than 100 registered members but in deference to those JDC members who had voted against the eighth register of the club, Frank Whitby and myself decided not to proceed with the acceptance of derivative replicars and specials with Jaguar engines such as the Lister-Jaguar, Ronart, and Kougar etc as we believed that with the furore by the so-called 'purists' initially it would be wise to have an acceptance of the works models to begin with before introducing these controversial makes. It was very important that the controlled specification was adhered to as near as possible to the Jaguar works models to avoid controversy.

At the end of September 1999 Frank Whitby resigned his position with the HRR and I took over as the magazine correspondent but on the 1st January 2003 I resigned as chairman as I was under intense pressure with the England/Hawthorn Memorial Appeal. Frank Whitby wished to resume his first love with classic motorcycles and grass track racing. This left only Terry Noble, the registrar/treasurer, as the only official until Paul Alcock was to become the new chairman/correspondent.

I refer the reader to the original origins and aims of the HRR, and it was imperative that these reproductions should *not* be described as kit cars, which the 750 Motor Club had famously introduced some years earlier sponsoring lightweight smaller capacity cars (i.e. Westfield, Caterham, Crossle, Sylva, etc., ad infinitum!), a completely different formula to the reproduction historic racing sports cars. This differential was not helped by the professional motor journalists and traders who used descriptive terms such as 'look-a-like', 'evocation', etc, and any other disparaging nomenclature they could think up. Finally to overcome this overall prejudice it maybe necessary to form a Historic Replicar Club, where control of the specification and quality standard will result in their acceptance that 'imitation is the sincerest form of flattery'.

In the Preface to this book, I highlight the detrimental affect of the self interest of certain officials with regard to Jaguar club motorsport which resulted subsequently in creating ill feeling between some members of both the Jaguar Drivers' Club and the Jaguar Enthusiasts' Club although some members like myself are members of both clubs.

At a time when Landrover Jaguar are producing more cars than ever before with a range of superb models it is important that the membership self interest should take a back seat so that we support their aspirations abroad particularly in Asia. Now owned by the Indian company Tata Motors, export sales are booking in India and China and we should support the Jaguar factory by establishing new official registers, forums, and areas in these countries.

The fragmentation of support in the United Kingdom will not encourage overseas commitment by Jaguar's customers in these new markets. Therefore there should be an amalgamation of the JDC and the JEC.

The Enthusiast Jaguar Drivers' Club could be both a classic car supporters club and a modern car supporters club with the former represented by the SS Register, the XK Register, the Mark VII/VIII/IX Register, Mark 1 & 2 Register, Classic S Type Register, the E-Type Register and the Historic Replicar Register; and the latter by the X-Type Forum, the X-350 Forum, the XJS Forum, the XF Forum, the XK8 Forum, the XJ Series Forum and the XF Forum with a new Forum representing the Jaguar Derivatives and Specials such as the Lister Jaguar, Kougar and Ronart, etc., and all new factory models to be represented by their own Forum.

For this development to succeed all members, particularly officials, would have to accept that the interest of the Jaguar Marque is paramount when I believe it would receive the support of Jaguar Cars Ltd and inspire them into supporting amateur Jaguar clubs abroad, but also cementing their relationship with customers in the UK and thereby creating a world-wide family of Jaguar owners which no other vehicle manufacturer would enjoy.

CHAPTER 18

England/Hawthorn Memorial Appeal

It was in April 1996 that I suggested in one of my articles in the club magazine that we should have a memorial to Mike Hawthorn, the first British World Champion driver in 1958. He was to die in a tragic road accident soon after. I met him a couple of times at race meetings and in particular at the European Grand Prix at Spa Francorchamps in Belgium in 1952 when I obtained his autograph in my pigskin cigarette case during practice.

A valuable piece of memorabilia. Pig skin cigarette case with autographs of famous racing drivers: Alberto Ascari, Mike Hawthorn, Luigi Villoresi, Jackie Stewart, Giuseppe Farina, Fangio, Martin Brundle, Mark Webber, Stirling Moss

Although I had seen F. R. W. 'Lofty' England on the pit counter at Le Mans over several years I did not meet him until much later when he joined the Jaguar Drivers' Club tours to continental destinations. He was such a keen supporter of all things Jaguar after he retired from being chairman and chief executive of Jaguar Cars Ltd that he should have been made president of the JDC but after a dispute with the then current chairman he relinquished contact with the club. As a regular correspondent in the *Jaguar Driver* magazine I received two copies each month and was able to send Lofty a copy over this period until he was reinstated with an honorary membership and regular magazines direct.

In recognition of my assistance in keeping him in touch with club affairs he invited my wife and myself to a restaurant in Most, Norway during the Scandinavian rally with his chauffeur Nils Abrahamson of the Jaguar Club of Denmark. We talked about his relationship with Mike Hawthorn when he was a Works driver after Mike's own father, Leslie Hawthorn had been killed a road accident. Lofty died in May 1995 at the age of eighty-four years. He was a man of genuine integrity. I was surprised he had not received an accolade from the government, first as manager of the winning Jaguar team at Le Mans and elsewhere right up to his appointment to the top job at Jaguar. I wrote to the Prime Minister's office earlier in 1995 for details of the PM's sponsorship scheme for awards to individuals who had been successful in British industry but unfortunately Lofty was to die before the application was completed. The first poster produced showing any surplus to be donated to BEN was later rescinded when I had a stroke and the surplus given to the Stroke Association in due course.

Sculptor David Annand works on the clay statue moulds for the England/Hawthorn Memorial. Photographer Alan Richardson

Following the article Nigel Webb had written to me supporting the idea of a memorial to Mike Hawthorn, as Lofty had now died I believed a memorial should be completed to recognise both these personalities and their special relationship.

However initially it was necessary to find a venue associated with both where statues could be erected in perpetuity. Lofty's ashes after cremation had been scattered at Silverstone where he had supervised the works Jaguar testing so I wrote to the secretary of the BRDC on the 21st November 1997 and it was taken up with the board of directors who basically turned the idea of a joint statue down. Meanwhile I obtained the names and addresses of all the Jaguar representatives throughout the world and wrote to them but received very little response. The appeal was going nowhere at this stage and although several Jaguar personalities expressed interest, nothing was done about it.

A selection of clay moulds by the sculptor taken from original clothing and equipment, i.e. 4 spoke steering wheel, Mike's helmet and brogue shoes. Photographer Alan Richardson

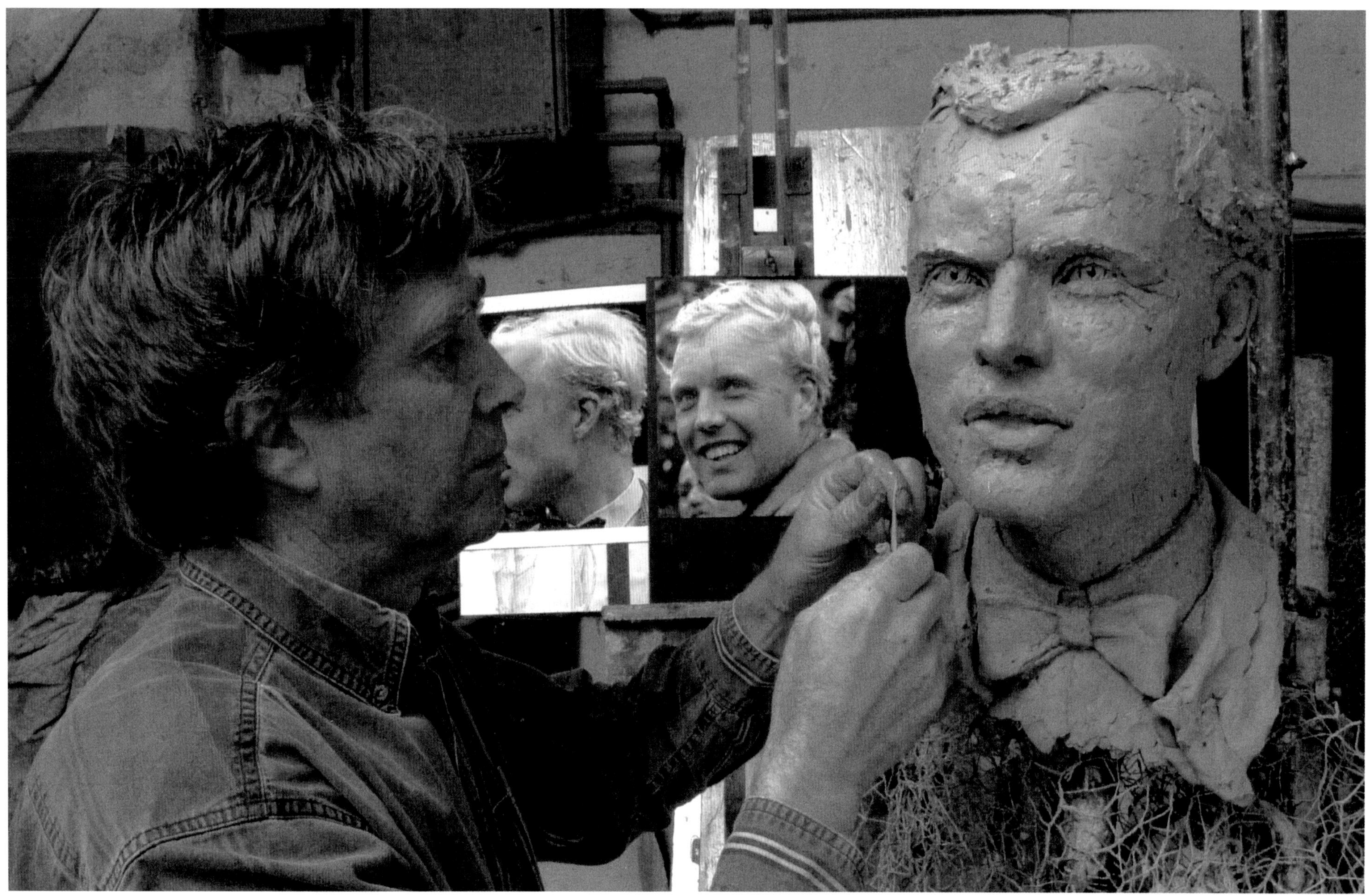

David Annand achieves a remarkable likeness of Mike Hawthorn for the clay mould using photographs. Photographer Alan Richardson

The memorial statue to Sir Douglas Bader sited in the Brooklands Garden at the Goodwood motor racing circuit

Other than supporters in Denmark the only other overseas Jaguar club to come forward in support was the Amicale Jaguar in France when Enrique Mistler, one of their officials, wrote to me advising how they thought a memorial was a great idea and how they always enjoyed his company when he visited them since 1987 and that they wished to collaborate with sending funds. Nothing was ever sent and it appears this offer was rescinded by their president Bernard Costen, who had won the 1964 Tour de France in a Mark II saloon; apparently after this victory he asked Jaguar to develop a lightweight version of this model which William Lyons declined. Without any explanation for this change of heart it seems his disappointment has affected his judgement some 40 years later!

I advised David Annand, the sculptor, that what I had in mind was two statues standing together in a posture which would reflect their special relationship. John Pearson, now an appeal committee member, had told me that one of the characteristics of Lofty when walking with a friend was to put his right arm through the left arm of the friend and this gave me the idea of the statue figure of Lofty with his right hand on Mike's left shoulder to reflect on the almost father and son relationship.

In August 2001 I read in the newspaper a report of the unveiling of a statue to Sir Douglas Bader at Goodwood so I wrote to the Earl of March asking him if he was prepared to have this dual statue at Goodwood. He replied on the 20th of August advising that he would be very pleased to meet up and discuss the proposal.

This was the breakthrough I needed and I immediately contacted David Annand in Scotland. David had completed all the statues at Mallory Park for the circuit owner Chris Meek. It was Chris who I had raced against in the 1970s and 80s who had given me David's name and address. However all statues at Mallory were life size and Lord March insisted on 110%.

Bader was five foot six so his increase in perspective was understandable but Lofty was six foot four and Mike six foot two so they would be giants at nearly seven feet and six foot ten respectively. In fact eventually their impact was outstanding but this increase in size cost the appeal substantially. If not Silverstone, Goodwood was a very good alternative because although Jaguar had not been particularly successful there it was Mike's home circuit where he had made his sensational debut. With the lack of support I was now looking round for benefactors but first an appeal committee was required.

John Pearson was a very old friend of Lofty's founder of Pearsons Engineering in Northamptonshire now run by his son Gary, a well known historic race car driver, who was to attend most if not all of the publicity events arranged and was invaluable in his help in view of my disability. Nigel Webb was a generous supporter of the appeal. A collector of Mike Hawthorn's memorabilia he owned the works D-Type Jaguar race car XKD505 which won the 1955 Vingt-Quatre du Mans driven by Mike and Ivor Bueb. Nigel was a successful racer of historic Jaguars.

So began an intensive period of publicity and promotion by myself and initially although all the connections were contacted again, the funding from abroad, particularly Lofty's adopted country Austria, where his wife still lived was very disappointing. The photograph shows the positioning of Mike and Lofty to depict their special relationship in real life and particularly the paternal stance of Lofty. The angle of the photograph is misleading because it appears that Mike is taller than Lofty whereas in real life Lofty was two inches taller. David Annand, with my own recommendations, had captured the 'devil-may-care' character of Mike which helped him to win the World Drivers Championship at the age of twenty-nine years in a decade when motor racing was very dangerous. The sort of character which epitomises the young Battle of Britain fighter pilots who flew from Westhampnett (Goodwood)

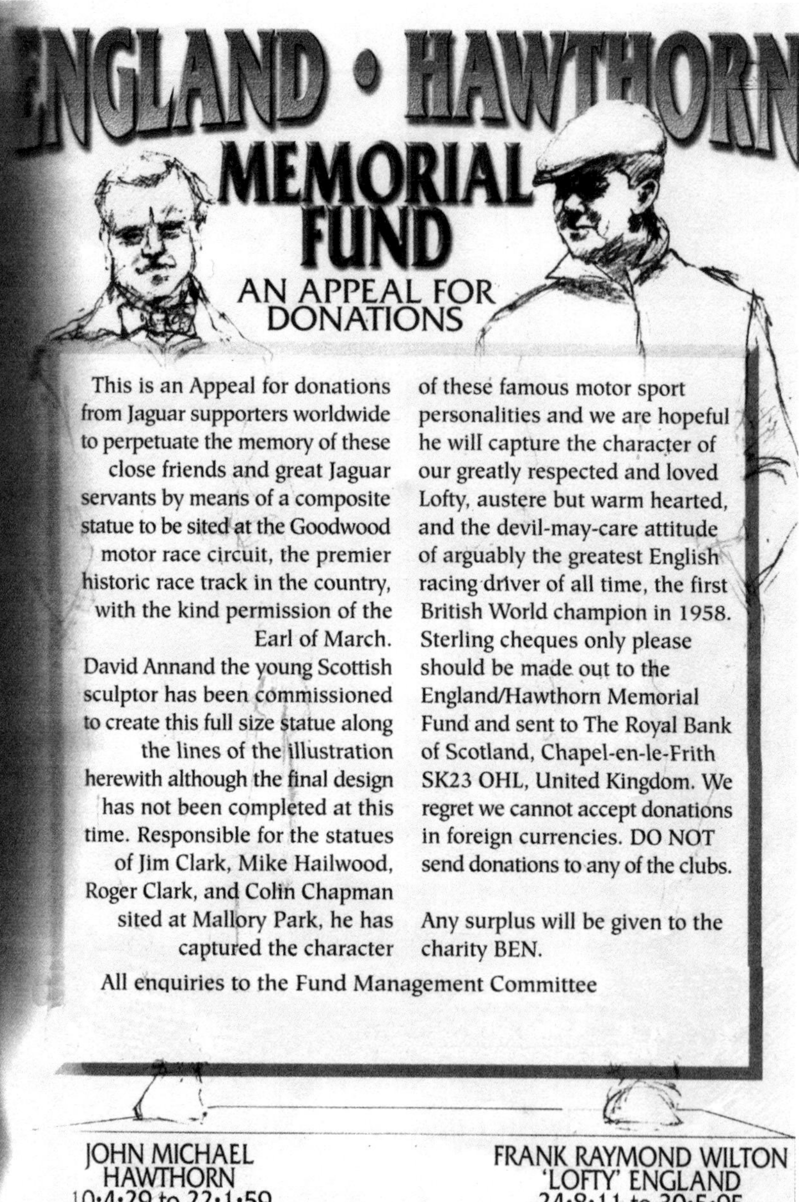

ENGLAND • HAWTHORN MEMORIAL FUND

AN APPEAL FOR DONATIONS

This is an Appeal for donations from Jaguar supporters worldwide to perpetuate the memory of these close friends and great Jaguar servants by means of a composite statue to be sited at the Goodwood motor race circuit, the premier historic race track in the country, with the kind permission of the Earl of March.

David Annand the young Scottish sculptor has been commissioned to create this full size statue along the lines of the illustration herewith although the final design has not been completed at this time. Responsible for the statues of Jim Clark, Mike Hailwood, Roger Clark, and Colin Chapman sited at Mallory Park, he has captured the character of these famous motor sport personalities and we are hopeful he will capture the character of our greatly respected and loved Lofty, austere but warm hearted, and the devil-may-care attitude of arguably the greatest English racing driver of all time, the first British World champion in 1958.

Sterling cheques only please should be made out to the England/Hawthorn Memorial Fund and sent to The Royal Bank of Scotland, Chapel-en-le-Frith SK23 OHL, United Kingdom. We regret we cannot accept donations in foreign currencies. DO NOT send donations to any of the clubs.

Any surplus will be given to the charity BEN.

All enquiries to the Fund Management Committee

JOHN MICHAEL HAWTHORN
10•4•29 to 22•1•59

FRANK RAYMOND WILTON 'LOFTY' ENGLAND
24•8•11 to 30•5•95

JAGUAR DRIVER MARCH

under the leadership of Douglas Bader only a decade earlier. Mike could always be identified by his polka-dot tie, his unique 1950s helmet with a white band, his stringback gloves, his brogue shoes and his short green jacket. The sculptor has completed these wonderfully accurately in view of the constraints of the bronze material used eventually. The Fund Management Committee were grateful to all those who loaned the original helmet and steering wheel for David Annand to copy.

Lofty on the other hand was eighteen years older than Mike and he had served in the RAF in the war in Bomber Command where he became a Lancaster instructor. Wearing his flat cap, he was well known to all British supporters at Le Mans. His jerkin and scarf show his wet weather garb and the armband carrying the official label supplied by the organisers, the Club de l'Ouest. In his left hand he is holding the four spoke steering wheel that was made especially for Mike by the Jaguar factory. This dedicated Jaguar man was authoritative in demeanour but much loved by all who knew him both at home and abroad. I believe he would have been very happy to have a memorial in association with Mike Hawthorn who had been killed twenty-six years earlier and for whom he had the highest regard and that he would have been pleased with its siting at Goodwood. Although the response from Jaguar supporters in the UK was encouraging but surprisingly even friends who accommodated Lofty on his visits to this country were very dilatory in their support. The three members of the committee decided to subsidise the cost of the initial instalment to get things cracking so that the moulds could be photographed and publicised generally.

So began a period of regular correspondence with David Annand and several visits to his studio in Kilmany, Scotland. Coincidentally in view of the motor racing connection there is a statue to Jim Clark, World Champion in a later era, sited in Kilmany because the Clark family farm was situated there although they had moved out of the area some years previously.

The clay mould for F.R.W. 'Lofty' England taken from his 1950s appearance. Photographer Alan Richardson

Presentation of the Jaguar X-Type saloon gifted to the England/Hawthorn Memorial Appeal by Jaguar Cars Ltd outside the factory offices in Brown's Lane, Coventry. Left to Right: Alan Hodge (Jaguar P.R.); Paul Alcock (Appeal team); Colin Cook (Jaguar P.R. Director); Ron Lea (Promoter); John Pearson (Appeal team); and Nigel Webb (Appeal team) standing by his exact replica of Mike Hawthorn's personal Jaguar saloon. Photographer Mike Cann

The appeal had been launched in March 2002, the funding of the memorial statues had not been realised. From the beginning my wife, Sheila, has acted as the secretary to the lottery involving filling in forms, dealing with bank cheques from supporters and suppliers, completing raffle ticket stubs (600 for Goodwood alone) folding leaflets, etc., etc., and finally removing staples from books of raffle tickets so that they could be separately placed in the rotating draw drum. The Funding Committee are grateful for her help which enabled them to arrive at a successful conclusion.

I always found Sir Nick Scheele when chairman and chief executive of Jaguar Cars Ltd to be very accessible, but he was now the number two to Billy Ford. Ford owned Jaguar Cars at the time. So I wrote to him at the Ford headquarters in Dearborn in the USA requesting a Jaguar car for the appeal to raffle. He replied immediately advising that whilst he agreed it was a worthwhile project, it was up to Jaguar to decide what they could do. I therefore wrote to Bob Dover, the chief executive of Jaguar/Land Rover at the time and asked him if Jaguar Cars would donate one of the new aluminium XJ saloons which we would raffle and so complete the funding. In the event, he authorised the gift of a 2-litre V6 X-Type sports saloon and this generous gift was announced in the November issue of *Jaguar Driver* Magazine. This unique car had an embossed plaque attached to the interior engraved in commemoration of these two legends and the rear bumper engraved. It was anticipated that the car would be displayed and the lottery commenced at the Classic Car Show on the 8th and 9th November with lottery tickets on sale at £2.00 each.

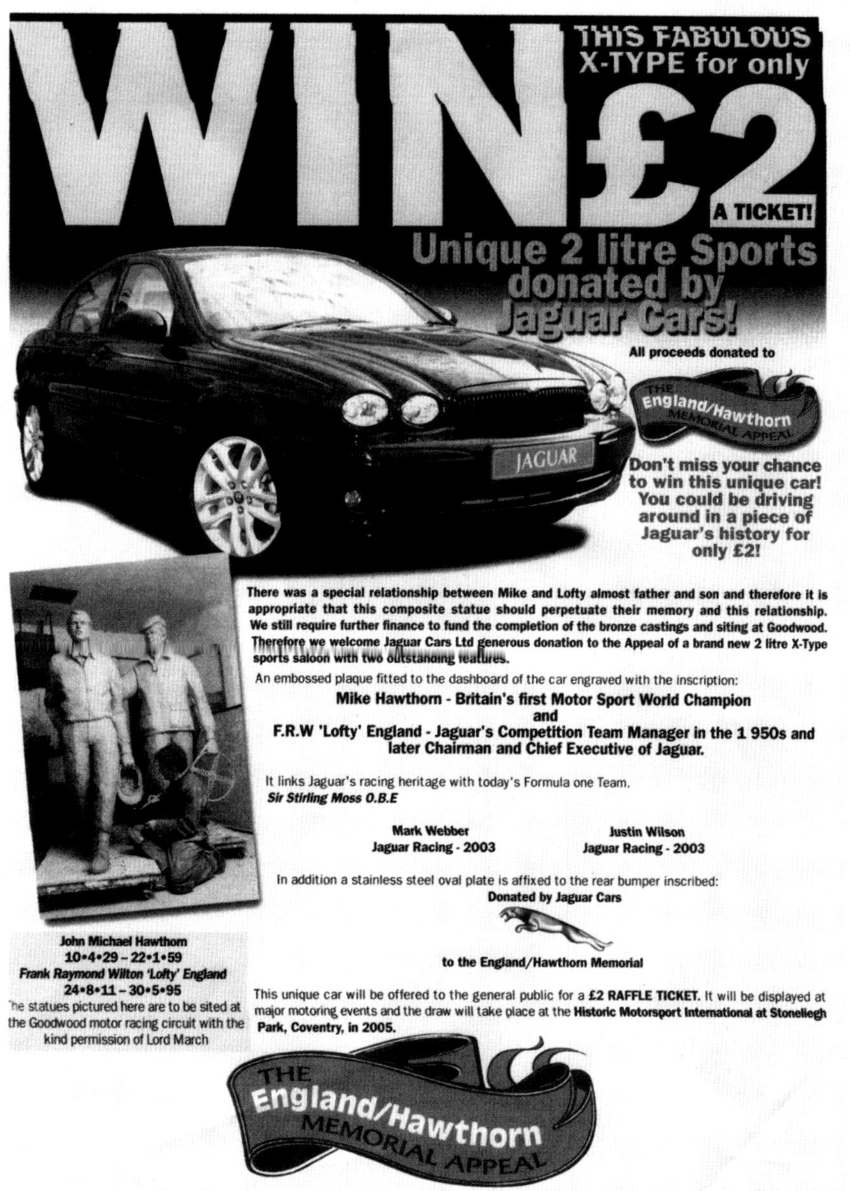

WIN THIS FABULOUS X-TYPE for only £2 A TICKET!

Unique 2 litre Sports donated by Jaguar Cars!

All proceeds donated to

THE England/Hawthorn MEMORIAL APPEAL

Don't miss your chance to win this unique car! You could be driving around in a piece of Jaguar's history for only £2!

There was a special relationship between Mike and Lofty almost father and son and therefore it is appropriate that this composite statue should perpetuate their memory and this relationship. We still require further finance to fund the completion of the bronze castings and siting at Goodwood. Therefore we welcome Jaguar Cars Ltd generous donation to the Appeal of a brand new 2 litre X-Type sports saloon with two outstanding features.

An embossed plaque fitted to the dashboard of the car engraved with the inscription:

Mike Hawthorn - Britain's first Motor Sport World Champion
and
F.R.W 'Lofty' England - Jaguar's Competition Team Manager in the 1 950s and later Chairman and Chief Executive of Jaguar.

It links Jaguar's racing heritage with today's Formula one Team.
Sir Stirling Moss O.B.E

Mark Webber
Jaguar Racing - 2003

Justin Wilson
Jaguar Racing - 2003

In addition a stainless steel oval plate is affixed to the rear bumper inscribed:
Donated by Jaguar Cars
to the England/Hawthorn Memorial

John Michael Hawthorn
10•4•29 – 22•1•59
Frank Raymond Wilton 'Lofty' England
24•8•11 – 30•5•95
The statues pictured here are to be sited at the Goodwood motor racing circuit with the kind permission of Lord March

This unique car will be offered to the general public for a **£2 RAFFLE TICKET.** It will be displayed at major motoring events and the draw will take place at the **Historic Motorsport International at Stoneliegh Park, Coventry, in 2005.**

THE England/Hawthorn MEMORIAL APPEAL

Jaguar Driver Dec 2003 **31**

Earlier that year when it looked as though funding would not be realised we were joined on the committee by Paul Alcock who used his computer knowledge to enquire if finance was available from the Heritage Lottery Fund, but we were told that they only helped to conserve and restore existing heritage and referred us to the Arts Council, England. They were unable to help either because they did not look upon this composite statue as a work of art.

CHAPTER 19

The Lottery: The Beginning of the End

It was now necessary to register with the Gaming Board of Great Britain, but we were not able to sell tickets at the Classic Motor Show as expected because it could not be registered in time. However, in the meantime, David Annand invited me to join him at the unveiling of the John Surtees memorial at Mallory Park which statue David had sculptured as he had all the others. I had an interesting conversation with Chris Meek whilst there and he later advised in a letter dated the 28th of August on Mallory Park Estate headed paper, that if I had approached him originally, he would have been prepared to site the composite statues at his circuit and would have paid for them in full! As all his statues were life size, two giants at nearly seven foot would have had to be sited in a special area away from the others which I am quite sure he would have accommodated. However, it was too late.

Now that we had been gifted the raffle car, it was necessary to arrange for a trailer with the capacity to carry such a large saloon for display at shows throughout the country. I had my race car trailer, but this was not up to the task. I therefore approached Moorland Classic Cars at Ipstones, Stoke-on-Trent who agreed to loan me their heavy duty car carrying trailer. I had the ideal towing vehicle, a 1996 4.6-litre V8 petrol Range Rover which had LPG fitted, but the mileage involved was very substantial.

Prior to applying for a lottery licence, I contacted Graham Searle the general manager of the Jaguar Enthusiast Club which had raffled eighteen second-hand cars since their founding in 1984 and suggested we did a joint lottery promotion in which we would require a guaranteed £35,000.00. We would do all the transporting of the raffle car and our committee would attend all the events at which it would be displayed. At the time they were having a successful raffle of the footballer Michael Owen's Jaguar X-Type saloon and had accumulated some £40,000.00 with excessive transport costs. Graham took it up with the club directors, but they thought the reserve of £35,000.00 was too much and they bought a second-hand Jaguar XK8. In fact, the amount we would eventually have required was £20,000.00, but I had to aim high to be sure to complete funding.

The Gaming Board of Great Britain understandably require comprehensive details of the prospective promoter including an enhanced disclosure, when a sample of the £2.00 raffle ticket had to be presented and the total face value expected to be sold, in our case £50,000.00. This application was dated 11th November 2003 with the date of the first ticket sales in January 2004. The registration fee was £4,600.00. On the 14th October, the Fund Management Committee meeting at the Jaguar Daimler Heritage Trust Museum comprising R. V. Lea, N. R. Webb, J. Pearson and P. Alcock, had unanimously agreed to register the lottery and all its requirements and I was selected as the promoter and contact with the society. The beneficiaries of any surplus would be the charity the Stroke Association.

Sir Stirling Moss calls at final Exhibition stand to sign the painting The Ragged Edge *depicting the legendary race between Mike Hawthorn (Jaguar D-Type) and himself (Mercedes-Benz 300 SLR) at the 1955 Tourist Trophy race at Dundrod, N. Ireland*

The Certificate of Registration was dated 5th December 2003. We had now introduced a second and third prize. The former was a painting by Paul Dove which he called 'The Ragged Edge'. This was a 60 × 90 cm painting featuring Mike Hawthorn, Stirling Moss and Jean Behra at the hairpin in the Tourist Trophy Race at Dunrod in Northern Ireland in 1955. In this very evocative painting, Paul has captured the essence of the competition between the Jaguar D-Type and the Mercedes-Benz 300 SLR which had started at Le Mans in 1955 between Mike Hawthorn and Juan-Manuel Fangio. I had seen this painting publicised in a motoring magazine

Ron Lea in lone attendance promoting the sale of raffle tickets at the Brands Hatch race circuit

Three committee members promoting the sale of raffle tickets at Brands Hatch. Note the 2nd prize, the painting The Ragged Edge *behind John Pearson's head*

Completed bronze statues at the Edinburgh foundry showing the impact of the 110% to life size, Lofty's statue is 7ft tall

for the first time and immediately contacted the artist, Paul Dove in Cornwall, and bought the original unseen. Sir Stirling Moss was the driver of the Mercedes on this occasion and much later was to visit our stand at the Classic Car Show and sign the original. He commented that it looked as though he was beaten by Mike Hawthorn whereas, in fact, he was to pass the D-Type after his co-driver, the American John Fitch, had lost so much ground that he had to catch-up and re-pass to win the race. Consequently, Mike was on the 'Ragged Edge' to keep ahead to no avail. A valuable painting of the two greatest English racing drivers of all time. Pity it could not have been signed by both. The third prize was a montage of model Jaguars in a garage setting and had been donated by committee member Paul Alcock.

Roger Lewis, former garage manager of Arleigh (Northern) Ltd on visit from British Columbia with former boss Ron Lea selling raffle tickets at Goodwood race circuit

It was in December 2002 that I received the first invoice from Powderhall Bronze in Edinburgh. The three original committee members had agreed to subsidise the initial cost to get the moulding started so that photographs could be taken and publicised asap. David Annand had authorised Powderhall to do the bronze casting. However, it had been agreed by all parties that the cost would be paid in instalments and I visited the Powderhall factory on several occasions to monitor progress.

Meanwhile, the pressure was on to sell raffle tickets as quickly as possible and an advertisement was placed in the *Jaguar Driver* and *Jaguar Enthusiast Club* magazines, when books of tickets were sent to JDC Registers and Areas to sell individual tickets to their members. The first display of the raffle Jaguar was at the Wembley Classic Car Show in December 2003, and thereafter was trailered all over the country by myself for display at classic car shows, racing car venues and even the War & Peace Show in Kent.

It was vital to display the car wherever there was a chance of selling tickets and it was assumed that the War & Peace Show would attract a patriotic public attendance, hopefully inclined to support such a British appeal, but in fact it turned out to be very disappointing. There were many people parading, some in Nazi German uniforms, but mostly in allied and famous British regimental gear. It was so dusty that my compatriot, John Pearson, washed the display car several times in the day to keep it pristine.

However, it was an incident on the return journey which reminded me of the experience I had returning from Le Mans in 1952 in my father's Morris Model E van some fifty-two years earlier. Travelling along the M25 amongst very heavy traffic, I had a puncture in the front nearside trailer tyre. At the time, I was traversing one of the tunnels so could not stop, which effectively destroyed the tyre. Reaching a layby, I managed to pull off the motorway, but it was still very close to the streaming traffic. I contacted the RAC breakdown service who arrived with a truck with two personnel. They were clearly concerned at the heavy fast-moving vehicles, both cars and commercials, and at first contacted their office for a heavy lift vehicle to load the X-Type and trailer, but one was not immediately available. After I had pointed out that the trailer carried its own spare, one of the mechanics started to jack the trailer and car whilst the other stood well away from the traffic stream. When I asked him why he was taking up this position, he advised that I should do the same in case a French lorry driver should come too close and clip the stationary vehicles. I was very aware that he did not state a continental driver with a left-hand drive truck, but referred to a French driver. In 1952, I had wondered why the American Army truck drivers had been warned there was a French convoy on the road and be prepared for an incident. It seemed the French truck drivers had retained their infamous reputation for creating mayhem!

Throughout 2004, we displayed the raffle car at a dozen venues commencing with the Historic Motorsports International at Stoneleigh Park in February, Jaguar Spares Day (also at Stoneleigh) in March, VSCC Meeting at Silverstone in April, Brands Hatch Classic Festival in May, Silverstone again in July, Stamford Hall also in July and the Festival of Speed at Goodwood, Woodvale Show in August, the Classic Car Show at Holder also in August, followed by the Tatton Park Show later that month, the Goodwood Revival Meeting in September, followed by the Meeting at Donington Park.

It was during September that I reported the current position of the finances having reached a total of £40,000.00, £24,000.00 from donations and £16,000 from the sale of raffle tickets, leaving a balance of some £17,000.00 to complete the funding. With only five months to the draw anticipated to take place at the Historic Motorsport International at Stoneleigh Park, the pressure was on to obtain the final balance. The International E-Type Register were due to have a track day at the Goodwood Circuit on the 15th November, and they kindly asked the Fund Management Committee to attend ostensibly to display the Jaguar X-Type raffle car when Nigel Webb suggested he would loan his famous D-Type replica (1955 Le Mans winner driven by Mike Hawthorn and Ivor Bueb) to give passenger rides to interested supporters of the appeal and arranged for Norman Dewis, the legendary Jaguar works test driver to take these brave volunteers round the Goodwood race track at racing speeds. A DVD of Win Percy demonstrating this very same car called *Sideways in a D-Type* was also offered to participants free and Roger Gage, professional

Norman Dewis, legendary Jaguar driver, hands over the 1955 Le Mans winning D-Type to Gary Pearson and takes a well earned rest. Photographer Roger Gage

Gary Pearson gives another supporter a run in the 1955 Le Mans D-Type owned by committee member Nigel Webb. Ron Lea surveys the scene. Photographer Roger Gage

photographer, took stills of each passenger co-pilot to record their memorable participation, also free of charge. This wonderful opportunity of a lifetime depended upon a donation to the appeal of a book of raffle tickets (twenty-five) at £2.00 each ticket, a total of £50.00.

It was a busy day for Norman, who at the age of eighty-four years took twenty donors several fast laps and when he came into the pits for a rest, Gary Pearson took over to satisfy another eight eager supporters. A total of some £1400.00 in donations, although Nigel's famous car required a new clutch by the end of the day.

This had been so successful that I approached the organisers of the following Aintree Festival who were going to open the Aintree Grand Prix Circuit after some forty years and they agreed to co-operate although they could not give us the same track time. Nigel agreed, however, to loan his early classic C-Type as well as the D-Type, and the committee member, John Pearson, agreed to loan his Lister-Jaguar also. Therefore, although the track time had been reduced, the increased participating race cars enabled us to increase the number of passenger rides resulting in a return of some £3000.00 with drivers Norman Dewis, Gary Pearson, John Pearson and Ben Cussons (Ben is one of the Cussons soap family) who kindly submitted his own Jaguar C-Type when Nigel's had brake trouble.

We displayed the raffle car at the Autosport International Exhibition at the NEC in January and, following this with the gifts from benefactors, the funding was completed with just the Portland Stone plinth to be finalised before the composite statues could be sited in the Brooklands Garden at Goodwood.

I therefore wrote to Bob Dover, the retired former chief executive of Jaguar/Land Rover who authorised the generous gift of the raffle car to ask him to draw the winning tickets at the February show to which he agreed.

It had been some four years since the appeal had been launched and the draw took place at the Second Historic Motorsport Show at Stoneleigh Park, Coventry on the 26th February 2005 when the X-Type Jaguar saloon was displayed for the last time. The well known journalist, Marcus Pye (editor in charge at *Autosport*) introduced myself as the promoter of the appeal and Bob Dover took out consecutively the three prize tickets from the rotated raffle barrel. The winners were announced, but only two were present, but we were able to telephone the main prize winner. The raffle car had to be returned to the factory for refurbishing and eventually handed over by myself and John Pearson at a main Jaguar dealer in Coventry. Unfortunately, the Jaguar/Heritage Trust was not able to replicate the official presentation by the Jaguar factory to the appeal committee. This was disappointing to Mr Frazier and his family, who had the raffle car winning ticket, and to the appeal committee who expected a formal presentation to the winner after the Jaguar factory had gifted the X-Type saloon outside their offices originally. Some time later, committee member Nigel Webb advised me that John Maries, the Managing Director of Jaguar Daimler Heritage Trust, had expressed an interest in storing the clay moulds for the England/Hawthorn composite statue with a view to possibly erecting a replica at their new address. The foundry advised that the moulds would be destroyed eventually as they had no storage room.

CHAPTER 20

The Unveiling of the England/Hawthorn Memorial Statues

Following a meeting with Lord March, he recommended a company in Chichester to do the groundwork and base/plinth in Portland stone. Soon after I called on the Cathedral Works Company to discuss our requirements. Lord March also asked his architects, Beardsmore Associates, to co-operate with the appeal committee to finalise the inscriptions on the plinth of the composite statue. It was at this same meeting that he recommended the historian Doug Nye should be involved whereas, in retrospect, I believe the motorsport journalist, Simon Taylor, would have been more appropriate because of his connection with Jaguar.

In the event, although the unveiling was scheduled for 12 noon and had been listed in the programme, Doug Nye urged Charles March to commence procedures well before this time which resulted in several supporters being disappointed in being too late for the unveiling. In his speech, Doug Nye praised the two outstanding personalities we were commemorating, and recalled the time he had an encounter with Mike Hawthorn in his Jaguar when he knocked him off his bike!

The unveiling took place on the 16th September, 2005, during the Goodwood Revival weekend and I arranged for invitations to be sent out to all the benefactors and supporters with detailed instructions. A special invitation was sent to Jane Fletcher, Lofty's daughter, and to Jean Ireland who as Jean Howarth was Mike Hawthorn's fiancée at the time of his death.

The Earl of March commences the unveiling procedure.
Photographer Roger Kemp

The composite statue of the Jaguar legends sited in the Brooklands Garden at the Goodwood racing circuit. Photographer Roger Kemp

Unfortunately, no instructions had been given to the clerk of the course to stop race cars practising so that the speeches given by Lord March, Doug Nye and Ole Sommer of Denmark, an old friend of Lofty's, could not be heard by many of the large crowd assembled in the Brooklands Garden. This was particularly sad for Ole Sommer, who had travelled especially from Denmark for this event, but I was able to have his speech published later in the Jaguar Drivers' Club magazine. Several invited guests complained to me at the time.

The statues are sited in an ideal position overlooking the race car assembly area on the Richmond Lawn and unveiled in the presence of many of their famous contemporaries, including Brian Lister of Lister Jaguar; Norman Dewis, for many years the Jaguar Works test driver and, more recently, race driver personalities Win Percy, Touring Car and Sportscar champion and Grand Prix driver Johnny Herbert.

The inscriptions on the plinth of the composite statute is as follows:

Plinth Front

centre in large capitals:	MAY THEIR FAME LIVE FOREVER
airfield side, left:	Mike Hawthorn 1929-1959
	First British World Champion 1958
airfield side, right:	'Lofty' England 1911-1995
	Jaguar Competition Manager 1949-1956
circuit side:	Appeal benefactors: Ron Lea, John Pearson,
	Nigel Webb
	Benefactors: Jaguar Cars Ltd, Lucas Huni,
	Ole Sommer,
	Clive Brandon, The Earl of March
rear:	Supporters: P. Alcock, J. Butterworth,
	Members of the JDC,
	XK Register, E-type Register, J.E.C. Jaguar Club
	of Denmark

Sculptor David Annand, Promoter Ron Lea and Committee member Nigel Webb stand by the composite statue, Goodwood. Photographer Roger Kemp

The final inscription detail can be seen on the statue including: David Annand – Sculptor. It had been nearly ten years since the idea of a commemorative statue to these two great English legends originated in my mind, and the subsequent trials and disappointments were forgotten when the unveiling took place. They stand in perpetuity at the Goodwood Race Circuit and I recommend all motorsport followers to visit and admire them in the Brooklands Garden. It was of great satisfaction to myself that there was a funding surplus and I was able to send a donation for £8,000.00 to the Stroke Association.

Incidentally, my wife, who is a successful crossword solver, has over the years been able to suggest names for companies and projects (i.e. Ascot and Encore) and in this instance, the most appropriate heading for the composite statue, i.e. 'May their fame live forever'.

The lottery licence had been valid for three years and as it was issued on the 5th December 2004, we had only had the use of it for fifteen months. On the 25th April, 2005, I offered the balance of the twenty-one months to the Jaguar Drivers' Club at a pro-rata cost of £3066.00 on the understanding this would be donated to the appeal. It was a cheap opportunity to become involved in the annual raffle of a second-hand Jaguar. However, I received a reply from the company secretary Kathy Beech, who stated that the club directors advised that the club was not in a position to accept my offer. I subsequently offered the remaining licence period to the XK register and the E-Type register, but both turned it down, understandably, in view of the minority register membership interest. If the main club with its much greater membership were not interested, its success in monetary terms was unlikely. However, even with the proposed donation to the appeal, it would have been a good start for an annual raffle in the future.

Jean Ireland stands in front of her former fiancé Mike Hawthorn and Jane Fletcher in front of her father Lofty England after the unveiling on the Richmond lawn in the Goodwood Brooklands Garden. Photographer Roger Kemp

Former race driver Peter Sutcliffe and committee member John Pearson in his racing overalls, Goodwood unveiling. Photographer Roger Kemp

Committee officials Nigel Webb, Paul Alcock and Ron Lea, Goodwood unveiling. Photographer Roger Kemp

Acknowledgements

I wish to acknowledge and thank the four members of the appeal committee, including my wife as secretary and John Pearson, Nigel Webb and Paul Alcock. John was very helpful in the logistics of the transport of the Jaguar X-Type raffle car to all the venues when it was physically impossible for myself to load and unload this saloon car, always attending the shows displaying the car and making sure it was always presentable and in pristine condition whilst promoting the sale of raffle tickets enthusiastically amongst his historic and classic car friends. Nigel was the epitome of generosity in the loan of his famous Le Mans winning Jaguar D-Type and valuable memorabilia. His company Air Traders required his regular attention which prevented him from attending some of the displays, but his enthusiasm was unstinted. Paul was the last one to join the appeal committee and in spite of his full time job as an Engineering Director of the airline BMI still found time to join the promotion at several exhibitions as well as arranging storage and transport of the raffle car. He also contributed the third place raffle prize.

We attended twenty-two events with the raffle car from November 2003 until February 2005; the lowest sale of raffle tickets was a Gaydon at £260.00 and the highest at the Goodwood Festival of Speed at £3,942.00. In addition the 'rides' at Goodwood and Aintree amounted to £1,600.00 and £2,200.00 respectively. The transporting of the raffle car to the events where it was displayed was achieved with my 4.6 litre Range Rover and trailer, which completed 20,000 miles during the whole period – 10,000 on behalf of the appeal, of which 3,000 were towing miles and unfortunately the latter resulted in a major engine breakdown in due course.

My eightieth birthday party celebration in April 2011 was an opportunity to have the family photograph, although three grandchildren were not present. It was also a time when I was able to welcome other relations and friends including my elder brother and his family, whilst my sister and her husband were not able to attend for medical reasons. The many friends present mainly from my Jaguar connections were very welcome although there were others whom I would have liked to invite, but administratively were impossible to accommodate.

The extended Lea family - 4 children, 11 grandchildren and 3 great grandchildren. Ron's 80th birthday party, April 2011